FOOD TO GROW AND LEARN ON

Recipes, Literature, And Learning Activities For Young Children

by Grace Bickert

Incentive Publications, Inc.
Nashville, Tennessee

Illustrated by Gayle Seaberg Harvey
Cover by Marta Drayton
Edited by Leslie Britt

Library of Congress Catalog Card Number: 93-80020
ISBN 0-86530-282-0

PRINTED IN THE UNITED STATES OF AMERICA

Table of Contents

January

February

March

April

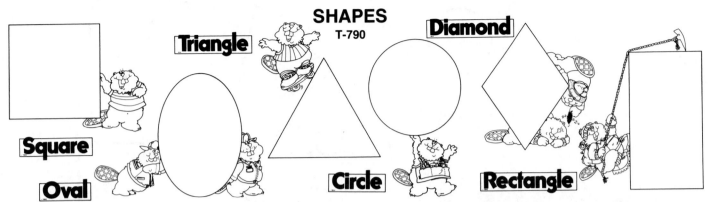

SHAPES
T-790

Square   Oval   Triangle   Diamond   Circle   Rectangle

OBJECTIVES

- To give practice in shape discrimination and color recognition.
- To provide multi-sensory opportunities to explore geometric forms.
- To encourage comparing shape similarities and differences.
- To provide a ready-to-use activity sheet reinforcing the bulletin board concepts.

ABOUT THE BULLETIN BOARD FIGURES

This SHAPES Bulletin Board set gives you the essentials for helping youngsters master which shape is which...with an exciting extra bonus! The basic colors are featured too!

These busy beavers prove that manipulating SHAPES and exploring colors can be lots of fun, and so do the activities you'll find below. Just post the ready-to-use cutouts and labels, take this Resource Guide in hand, and your shape study is underway! Some youngsters will be able to name the shapes in this set, and all will enjoy discussing what features make the shapes similar or different. They'll soon be taking a new look around the classroom at the floor, windows, ceiling tiles, clock faces, and even the triangles and circles of letters in the manuscript alphabet line. Take time to fully explore the shapes and use the Resource Guide activities to discover how fun and challenging shapes can be. Then pass out the activity sheet on page two of this Resource Guide, and let each youngster demonstrate his or her own shape and color know how!

SHAPE AWARENESS ACTIVITIES

1. **Body Shapes.** To get a real feel for geometric shapes, do bodily interpretations! Say, "Use your body to show me how you would look if you were a triangle." Too easy? Challenge with a riddle instead. They're fun to answer and fun to think up! Here's one: "I am thinking of a shape that has the same number of pointy corners as there are wheels on a tricycle. Indian teepees and some ice cream cones look like this shape. How would you look if you were this shape?"

2. **Stick-and-Stay Shape Learning Center.** Cut shapes galore from colored felt. Invite youngsters to explore, sort and classify them by shape and color on a felt-board background during free times.

3. **Cookie Cut-ups.** One way to the memory is through the tummy! Make and roll out a large batch of cookie dough. Everyone gets in on the act as youngsters cut the dough into basic shapes with cookie cutters or by tracing around cardboard patterns with butter knives. Name each shape, then decorate bake and eat!

4. **Crunchy Shapes.** Provide geometrically shaped crackers, together with cheese spreads and peanut butter. When youngsters match two cracker shapes correctly, the reward is to make a shape "sandwich" to eat!

5. **Clown Face Shapesters.** Combine the bulletin board shapes to produce as many unique and different clown faces as you have youngsters. Provide pre-cut construction paper shapes of all sizes and colors, or have youngsters cut their own. Encourage each person to use at least three different shapes to create hats, eyes, mouths, noses, ears, cheeks, hair, eyebrows, beards, freckles and even teeth!

6. **Puppet Pals.** Homemade puppets (for example, make Cindy Circle, Ted Triangle, Randy Rectangle, Dick Diamond, Ole Oval, etc.) are great attention grabbers for introducing shapes. Your library should be able to provide books and "how-to-do-it" guides for handcrafted puppets.

7. **Cover Sorting.** Size and shape matching becomes a real life puzzle with this hands-on activity using all the jars, bottles and boxes (each with a cover) you can collect. Spread the assortment of containers on one end of a table, and their covers on the other end. Puzzlers mix and match until they find the winning combinations.

8. **Tracing Shapes.** Finger-trace shapes in sand, mud, finger paint or clay. Chalk, crayons, pipe cleaners, string and building blocks are great shape-makers, too!

9. **Shape Relay.** Divide your group into relay teams and take a grandstand seat for the fun! Teams line up at one end of the room, each behind their own tape-on-the-floor "finish line." At the opposite end of the room are boxes (one box per team) containing several tagboard shapes, including the six represented on the bulletin board. One player - a Game Captain - calls a shape and the race is on! Example: "Triangle — on your mark, get set, GO!" The first person in each line races for his/her team's box, locates the shape and returns to the team with the shape in hand. The first correct shape across the finish line earns a point for that team. The next players on each team then race for another shape, etc. The high point team wins, and the game continues until all players have had a turn.

10. **Shape Take-Away.** Here's a game to shape up memories and build shape identification! You need construction paper geometric shapes. Players sit in a circle on the floor with the shapes spread out in the center for all to see. One player leaves the circle (or covers his/her eyes), while another player takes one shape from those on the floor and hides it. "It" returns (or opens the eyes) and gets two chances to guess which shape is missing. If correct, he or she chooses a new "It" and also hides the next shape. If not correct, he or she merely rejoins the circle, the teacher or leader selects a new "It" and a player to hide the shape, and the game continues.

Color:

☐ red   ◯ yellow

◯ purple   △ green

▭ blue   ◇ orange

Summer Months

Colors

ABC's

Storybook

Preface

Food To Grow and Learn On is a book of recipes, literature, and learning activities intended for preschool and early elementary school children. The activities and recipes presented in the book are appropriate for use in a school, home, child care center, or after-school cooking club setting.

For ease of use, this book has been organized in a calendar format for the entire school year, with the inclusion of sections on summer months, colors, storybooks, and the ABC's. Each month contains a host of thematic learning activities (literature-related activities, books to read, suggestions for ways to use the recipes in your daily lesson plan, games, fingerplays, art activities, classroom discussions, songs, etc.), a list of additional books related to the month's themes, and a series of recipes.

The recipes are tasty and easy and fun to make. Some do not require cooking; others can be prepared in the classroom using hot plates, electric skillets, crockpots, toaster ovens, and blenders. When cooking in the classroom, it is best to place children in small groups. This gives each child the opportunity to mix, grind, sift, and blend. You may want to invite parents to share this marvelous learning experience with their children by asking them to visit the classroom as guest chefs. Sending home recipes for children and parents to make together is also a terrific approach to getting children cooking and learning.

The book's activities link cooking with all areas of the classroom curriculum:

- **Cooking promotes the Language Arts** when recipes and hands-on activities are linked to storybook characters, poems, and creative writing experiences.

- **Cooking promotes Math skills** when children measure, estimate quantity and outcome, and graph favorite foods.

- **Cooking promotes Health and Science skills** when children are taught about boiling water and rising bread, when they see, taste, smell, hear, and feel a variety of foods, and when they learn about nutrition.

Cooking promotes Social Studies and History skills when children learn about the food and social customs of other cultures and races.

Cooking promotes Social skills when children learn to cooperate, to share, to accept responsibility, and to practice good manners. Cooking—and making a finished product—also instills in children a sense of pride and accomplishment which builds self-esteem.

Ignite your students' imagination and enthusiasm for learning with *Food To Grow and Learn On!*

September

SAFETY

It is important that children learn about safety at the beginning of the school year. Personal safety, bus safety, and fire safety need to be reviewed at all age levels. Consider the following activities:

■ Schedule a classroom visit by a local police officer or firefighter. You may wish to prepare for the visit by reading *Red Light, Green Light* by Margaret Wise Brown or *Fire! Fire!* by Gail Gibbons. A batch of **Traffic Light Cookies** (page 15) or **Matchstick Crackers** (page 15) makes a nice thank-you gift for your safety visitor. You may wish to make enough so that the police officer can take some back to the police station or the firefighter can take some back to the firehouse.

■ Art activity: Make Traffic Lights. You will need a half-gallon paper milk carton for each child and construction paper in white, red, green, and yellow. Each child will cover his or her milk carton with white construction paper. Cut 3″ circles from the red, green, and yellow construction paper and have each child glue one of each color in the appropriate place on the milk carton (red is on top, yellow in the center, and green on the bottom).

■ Preparing an **Edible Campfire** (page 16) is an effective way to teach children about outdoor fire safety. Serve the "campfire" with a glass of water—you should always have water near a campfire! A good book to accompany this activity is *Amelia Bedelia Goes Camping* by Peggy Parish.

■ Play a lively game of "Red Light, Green Light, Yellow Light, STOP." Line the children up side by side. One child, selected as the "caller," will walk forward several yards. Standing with his or her back to the other children, the caller will chant: "Red light, green light, yellow light, STOP." The caller turns around quickly after shouting "STOP." The children, meanwhile, try to creep up and cross the caller's line before he or she shouts "STOP." If the caller turns around and catches someone moving after the word STOP, that player must go back to the starting line. The first player over the caller's line becomes the next caller.

■ Read the story of "Little Red Riding Hood." Afterwards, ask the students to tell you all the safety rules that Little Red Riding Hood and Grandma didn't follow:
   1. Red Riding Hood stopped along the way even though her mother told her to go directly to Grandma's.
   2. Red Riding Hood talked to a stranger.
   3. Grandma left her door unlocked.
   4. Even though Red Riding Hood thought that Grandma looked strange, she didn't run away.

Children love discovering all the mistakes that Red Riding Hood made, and, of course, they love making claims that they would never do any of these things. **Little Red Riding Hood's Cookies for Grandma** (page 120) make a nice treat for all your safety-conscious students!

JOHNNY APPLESEED

The birthday of Johnny Appleseed (born John Chapman on September 26, 1774) ties in very nicely with the fall apple season. Excellent books about this folk hero are *Johnny Appleseed* by Stephen Kellogg and *Little Brother of the Wilderness: The Story of Johnny Appleseed* by Meridel LeSueur.

■ Students love taking walks and collecting leaves at the beginning of the fall season. Find some leaves from apple trees (or bring some in from elsewhere) and compare them to the other leaves you find. Allow leaves to dry inside magazines for several days. Make leaf rubbings by covering leaves with paper and rubbing crayons over the paper. The children will love the story *Red Leaf, Yellow Leaf* by Lois Ehlert and *The Fall of Freddie the Leaf* by Leo Buscaglia.

■ Share this popular fingerplay with your class:

> Away up high in an apple tree,
> *(Point up)*
> Two shiny apples smiled at me.
> *(Form two circles with fingers)*
> I shook that tree as hard as I could.
> *(Shake tree)*
> Down came the apples—m-m-m-m, were they good!
> *(Rub stomach)*

■ Make Apple Family Trees. Bring some apples into class (or you may be lucky enough to find some on the ground when you take your walk). Cut the apples in half. Use a crayon to draw brown tree trunks with large branches on construction paper. Dip the cut sides of the apples in red paint and use them to print onto the trees. Each child may print a number of apples that is the same as the number of people in his or her family. After the paint dries, use a black marker to print a family member's name on each apple print. You may display the Apple Family Trees during your school's Open House. They will be a tremendous success!

■ A delicious way to celebrate fall is to make **Applesauce** (page 16), **Waldorf Salad** (page 17), or **Cider Delighter** (page 17). Ask the students to bring in the apples—two per child is usually more than enough.

■ Some "appeal-ing" read-aloud books for times between apple activities are *Apple Pie* by Anne Wellington, *Rain Makes Applesauce* by Julian Schur, and *The Seasons of Arnold's Apple Tree* by Gail Gibbons.

ROSH HASHANA

Days of Awe by Eric Kimmel explores the meaning of Rosh Hashana (celebrated in the early fall—the first day of the Jewish month of Tishri). Susan Gold Purdy's book *Jewish Holidays* contains information plus craft ideas.

■ A sweet recipe such as **Frosted Grapes and Honeyed Apples** (page 18) is wonderful for the beginning of the Jewish New Year (Rosh Hashana) and signifies the heartfelt yearning for a sweet and happy year.

OTHER BOOKS FOR SEPTEMBER

Applebet by Clyde Watson.

Fire Fighters by Rob Maass.

A Tree Is Nice by Janice Udry.

Rosh Hashana by Barbara Diamond Goldin.

Safety Can Be Fun by Munro Leaf.

TRAFFIC LIGHT COOKIES

- ½ cup butter
- ½ cup margarine
- 1 cup sugar
- 2 eggs
- 1 teaspoon vanilla
- 3½ cups flour
- 1 teaspoon baking powder
- ¼ teaspoon salt
- red, yellow, and green coated chocolate candies

Preheat oven to 375°. Cream butter, margarine, and sugar in a large bowl. Beat eggs and vanilla into the mixture. In a separate bowl, mix the flour, baking powder, and salt. Add the flour mixture to the creamed butter and sugar. On a floured surface, roll or pat the dough to a thickness of about ¼″, and cut into 1″ x 4″ rectangles. (The bottom of a rectangular spice tin works well as a make-shift cookie cutter.) Place dough on greased cookie sheets and let children press the coated chocolate candies onto the dough to resemble traffic lights. Bake for 8 to 10 minutes. Take care not to let the cookies get too brown.

MATCHSTICK CRACKERS

- 1½ cups flour
- 1 teaspoon salt
- ¼ teaspoon cayenne powder
- ½ cup (1 stick) butter or margarine
- 1½ cups cheddar cheese, grated
- 3 to 4 tablespoons ice water
- ¼ cup paprika

Preheat oven to 425°. Sift together the flour, salt, and cayenne powder. Cut in the butter or margarine with a pastry blender until the mixture has achieved a crumbly consistency. Add grated cheese and ice water to the dough. Stir until mixture forms a ball. Roll out the dough about ¼″ thick, and cut dough into sticks approximately the size of your middle finger. Place the sticks on ungreased cookie sheets and bake for 15 minutes. Measure ¼ cup paprika into a small bowl and dip one end of each stick into the paprika. (Yield: approximately 60 sticks.)

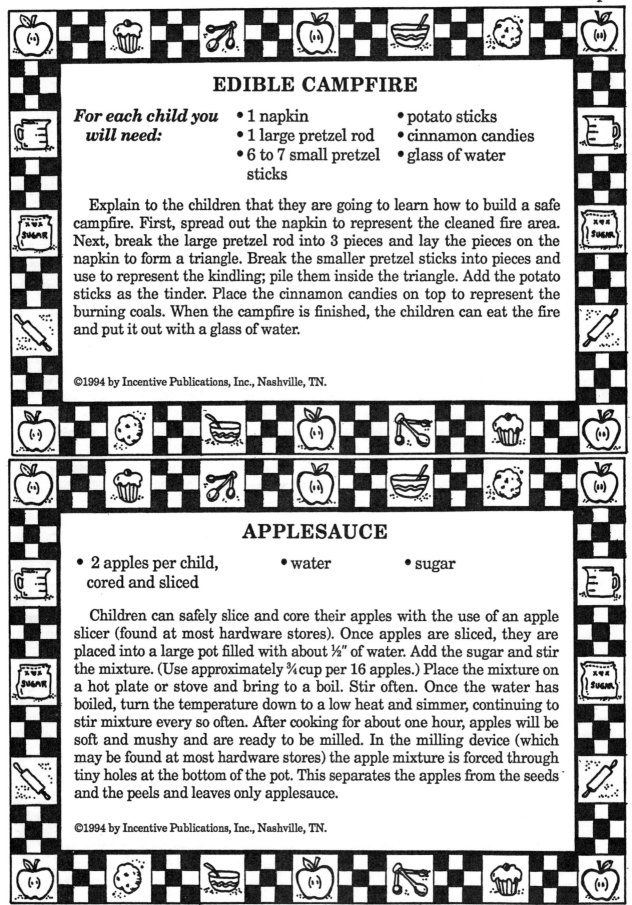

EDIBLE CAMPFIRE

For each child you will need:
- 1 napkin
- 1 large pretzel rod
- 6 to 7 small pretzel sticks
- potato sticks
- cinnamon candies
- glass of water

Explain to the children that they are going to learn how to build a safe campfire. First, spread out the napkin to represent the cleaned fire area. Next, break the large pretzel rod into 3 pieces and lay the pieces on the napkin to form a triangle. Break the smaller pretzel sticks into pieces and use to represent the kindling; pile them inside the triangle. Add the potato sticks as the tinder. Place the cinnamon candies on top to represent the burning coals. When the campfire is finished, the children can eat the fire and put it out with a glass of water.

APPLESAUCE

- 2 apples per child, cored and sliced
- water
- sugar

Children can safely slice and core their apples with the use of an apple slicer (found at most hardware stores). Once apples are sliced, they are placed into a large pot filled with about ½" of water. Add the sugar and stir the mixture. (Use approximately ¾ cup per 16 apples.) Place the mixture on a hot plate or stove and bring to a boil. Stir often. Once the water has boiled, turn the temperature down to a low heat and simmer, continuing to stir mixture every so often. After cooking for about one hour, apples will be soft and mushy and are ready to be milled. In the milling device (which may be found at most hardware stores) the apple mixture is forced through tiny holes at the bottom of the pot. This separates the apples from the seeds and the peels and leaves only applesauce.

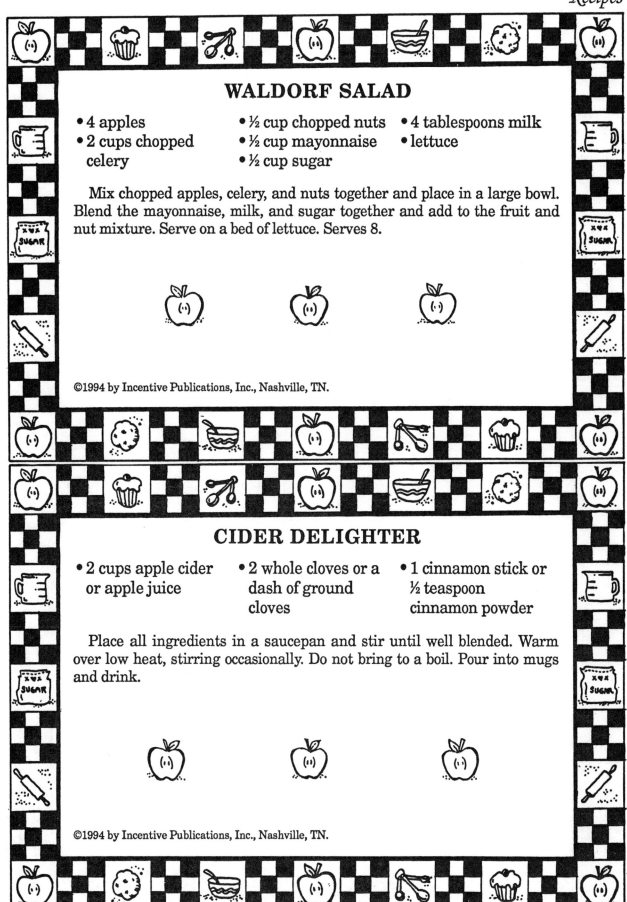

WALDORF SALAD

- 4 apples
- 2 cups chopped celery
- ½ cup chopped nuts
- ½ cup mayonnaise
- ½ cup sugar
- 4 tablespoons milk
- lettuce

Mix chopped apples, celery, and nuts together and place in a large bowl. Blend the mayonnaise, milk, and sugar together and add to the fruit and nut mixture. Serve on a bed of lettuce. Serves 8.

CIDER DELIGHTER

- 2 cups apple cider or apple juice
- 2 whole cloves or a dash of ground cloves
- 1 cinnamon stick or ½ teaspoon cinnamon powder

Place all ingredients in a saucepan and stir until well blended. Warm over low heat, stirring occasionally. Do not bring to a boil. Pour into mugs and drink.

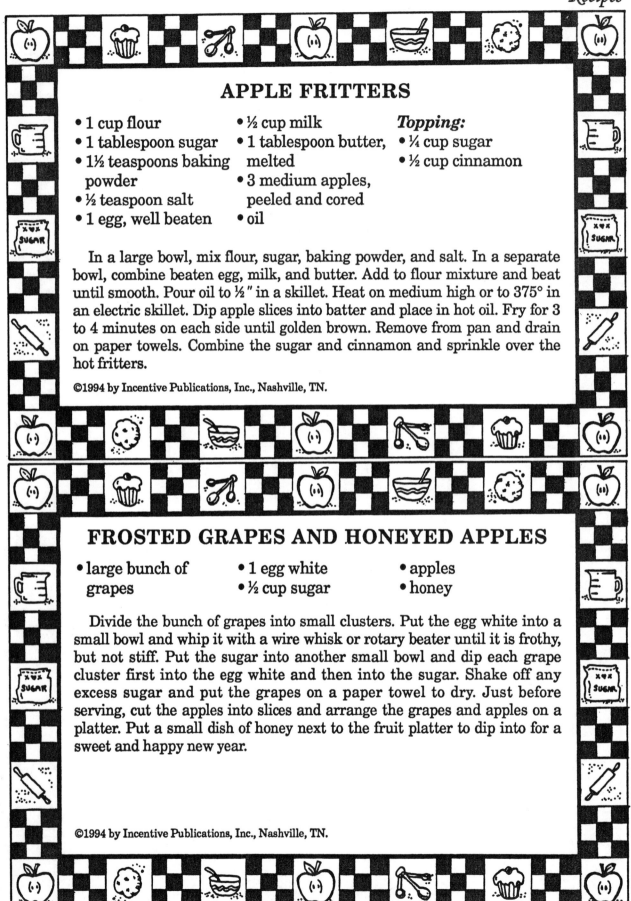

APPLE FRITTERS

- 1 cup flour
- 1 tablespoon sugar
- 1½ teaspoons baking powder
- ½ teaspoon salt
- 1 egg, well beaten

- ½ cup milk
- 1 tablespoon butter, melted
- 3 medium apples, peeled and cored
- oil

Topping:
- ¼ cup sugar
- ½ cup cinnamon

In a large bowl, mix flour, sugar, baking powder, and salt. In a separate bowl, combine beaten egg, milk, and butter. Add to flour mixture and beat until smooth. Pour oil to ½″ in a skillet. Heat on medium high or to 375° in an electric skillet. Dip apple slices into batter and place in hot oil. Fry for 3 to 4 minutes on each side until golden brown. Remove from pan and drain on paper towels. Combine the sugar and cinnamon and sprinkle over the hot fritters.

FROSTED GRAPES AND HONEYED APPLES

- large bunch of grapes
- 1 egg white
- ½ cup sugar
- apples
- honey

Divide the bunch of grapes into small clusters. Put the egg white into a small bowl and whip it with a wire whisk or rotary beater until it is frothy, but not stiff. Put the sugar into another small bowl and dip each grape cluster first into the egg white and then into the sugar. Shake off any excess sugar and put the grapes on a paper towel to dry. Just before serving, cut the apples into slices and arrange the grapes and apples on a platter. Put a small dish of honey next to the fruit platter to dip into for a sweet and happy new year.

LOKSHEN KUGEL (NOODLE PUDDING)

- 2 eggs
- 1 tablespoon granulated sugar
- ¼ teaspoon ground nutmeg
- 2½ cups cooked broad noodles
- 1 tablespoon vegetable oil
- 1 cup unsweetened apple juice
- ½ cup dark or golden raisins
- ¼ cup chopped walnuts or pecans

Beat the eggs and sugar until fluffy. Add the remaining ingredients (except the nuts) to the egg mixture. Pour into a well-oiled 2-quart casserole dish or an 8″ baking pan. Sprinkle the nuts on top. Bake at 350° for 40 to 50 minutes, or until browned.

SWEET AND SOUR GREEN BEANS

- 1 package frozen green beans (10 oz.)
- ½ cup water
- 1 bay leaf
- 4 whole cloves
- 2 tablespoons red or white vinegar
- 1 tablespoon margarine
- 1 tablespoon sugar

Combine the beans, water, bay leaf, and cloves in a saucepan and cook until the beans are tender. Drain the excess water and add the vinegar and margarine. Cook 3 more minutes. Remove the bay leaf and cloves and sprinkle with sugar. Serves 4.

October

COLUMBUS DAY

Kids love to learn about the adventures of Columbus and his search for new lands in the Western Hemisphere. Introduce some facts and some discussion questions about Columbus's voyages, as in the following paragraph.

■ "In fourteen-hundred and ninety-two, Columbus sailed the ocean blue." What else can you think of that rhymes with blue? How many things can you write down that are blue in color? When Columbus left on his voyage, people thought that they would never see him again because they believed that the world was flat. What do you think would happen if the world really were flat? Why was Columbus's trip across

the ocean so difficult? What do we have today that Columbus didn't have when he was a boy? The *Santa Maria* was the only ship of the first three that left Spain to arrive in the new land. This ship stayed afloat. What else besides a boat floats? More facts about Columbus can be found in *Columbus* by Edgar and Ingri D'Aulaire.

■ After discussing Columbus Day, serve a **Columbus Day Salad** (page 24), or let the children make **Egg Sailboats** (page 24).

HALLOWEEN

Children love being scared during Halloween. Introduce these activities to your classroom for chills and thrills:

■ Halloween songs are always fun, but they become even more enjoyable when children can create their own lyrics to popular tunes. For example, the tune of "Have You Seen the Muffin Man?" lends itself to such lyrics as "Have you seen the scary ghost, scary ghost, scary ghost? Have you seen the scary ghost that lives on Boo-Boo Lane?" Children can also sing "Have you seen the hairy spider, the hairy spider, the hairy spider? Have you seen the hairy spider that lives in the web on the wall?" After children have written their own songs, help them write their new lyrics on a sheet of paper to take home. Top the day off by making no-bake **Spider Cookies** (page 25). These cookies will send shivers of delight up and down the children's spines!

■ Eric Carle's book *The Very Busy Spider*, Margaret Bloy Graham's *Be Nice to Spiders*, and the ever-popular story of "Little Miss Muffet" make wonderful reading during this special time of year.

■ After several lessons on shapes and colors, make a tasty **Jack-o-Lantern Pizza** (page 25). With its triangular nose, round eyes, and green pepper stem, this pizza makes a healthful alternative to traditional Halloween candy.

■ For pumpkin fun, give each child a piece of paper with a pumpkin shape drawn on the front side of the paper and a certain number of pumpkin seeds drawn on the back. Instruct the children to draw triangle, circle, and square shapes to turn their pumpkins into jack-o-lanterns. When all of the drawings are completed, tell the children to hold their papers up to the light and look for a surprise. (They will be able to see the pumpkin seeds that are drawn on the other side of the paper.) Ask each child to count the number of seeds in his or her picture.

■ Books about pumpkins are especially appropriate during the month of October. Two favorites are *The Pumpkin People* by Daniel and Maggie Caravagno and *Pumpkin, Pumpkin* by Jeanne Titherington.

■ An at-home activity involves parents giving their children a certain amount of pumpkin seeds and asking the children to count the seeds. Encourage children to bring to class their pumpkin seeds after they have dried. Pumpkin seeds come in handy for a variety of art projects: the seeds are big enough for small fingers to handle, and they can be glued onto paper to make art collages. Nice plump pumpkin seeds are washed and baked to make a **Crunchy Pumpkin Seed** (page 27) snack.

■ After reading Wende and Harry Devlin's *Old Black Witch* try the recipe for delicious **Spellbinding Blueberry Pancakes** (page 27). You can swirl the pancake batter as you pour it onto the skillet; children will enjoy guessing what the odd designs look like.

■ A super Halloween activity involves creating a list of ingredients that might go into a Witches' Brew. For children who are not yet reading, glue pictures or actual objects to a piece of posterboard. Some suggestions include pebbles, twigs, acorns, leaves, pine cones, blades of grass, dead flowers, etc. Children can participate by collecting items of their own choosing and placing them in paper bags to share with the class. After all of the items have been collected, it can be fun to have children rename all of the objects they found: leaves become bat wings, acorns turn into frog warts, and green blades of grass become witch's hair. If your school grounds do not have an area filled with trees, pine cones, etc., you can plan ahead and hide the items for the children to find. After all of the fun, you can create your own Witch's Brew by stirring up some **Vegetable Chowder** (page 109).

OTHER BOOKS FOR OCTOBER

The Ghost with the Halloween Hiccups by Stephen Mooser.

Halloween with Morris & Boris by Bernard Wiseman.

That Terrible Halloween Night by James Stevenson.

Who Sank the Boat? by Pamela Allen.

COLUMBUS DAY SALAD

Legend has it that Columbus brought the pineapple to the New World.

- 1 cup pineapple
- 1 cup banana
- ½ cup coconut, grated
- 1 cup orange slices

Mix all of the ingredients together and serve.

EGG SAILBOATS

- 1 dozen eggs, hard boiled
- ½ cup mayonnaise
- 1 teaspoon mustard
- 2 dozen toothpicks
- sheets of paper

Shell eggs, slice in half, and remove yolks. Combine the egg yolks with mayonnaise and mustard and return to the hollow of each egg. Tape small triangles of paper to toothpicks and stick them in the egg halves.

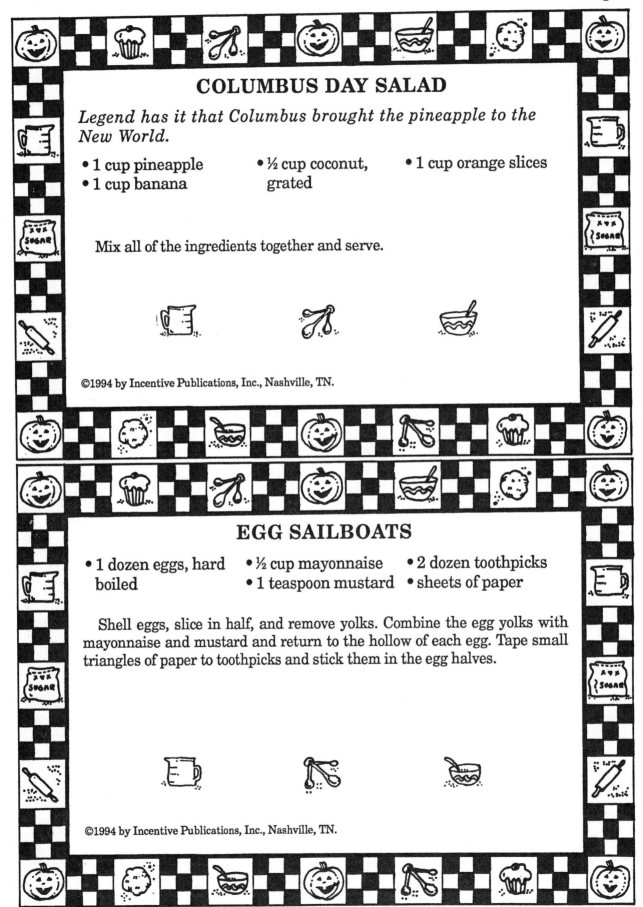

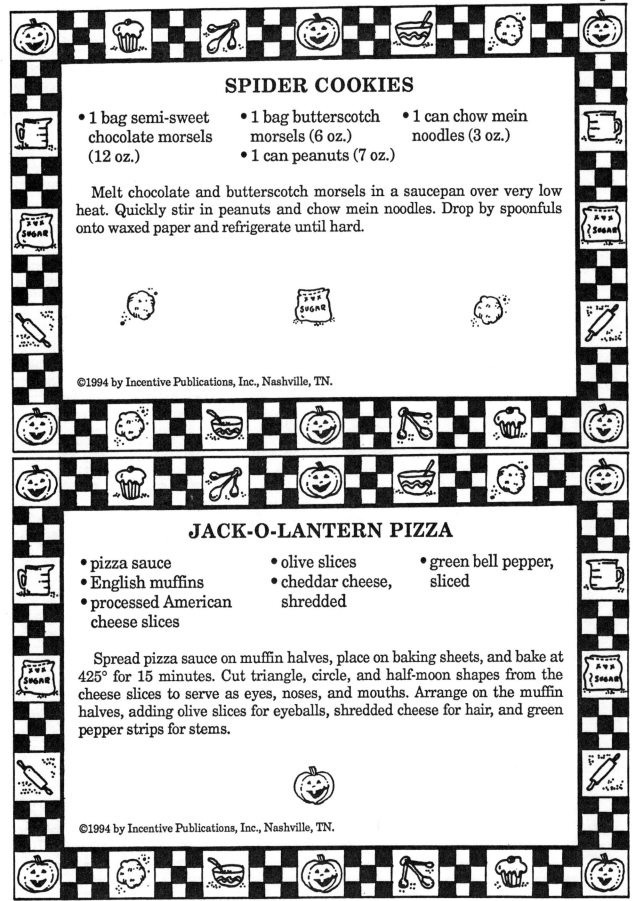

SPIDER COOKIES

- 1 bag semi-sweet chocolate morsels (12 oz.)
- 1 bag butterscotch morsels (6 oz.)
- 1 can peanuts (7 oz.)
- 1 can chow mein noodles (3 oz.)

Melt chocolate and butterscotch morsels in a saucepan over very low heat. Quickly stir in peanuts and chow mein noodles. Drop by spoonfuls onto waxed paper and refrigerate until hard.

JACK-O-LANTERN PIZZA

- pizza sauce
- English muffins
- processed American cheese slices
- olive slices
- cheddar cheese, shredded
- green bell pepper, sliced

Spread pizza sauce on muffin halves, place on baking sheets, and bake at 425° for 15 minutes. Cut triangle, circle, and half-moon shapes from the cheese slices to serve as eyes, noses, and mouths. Arrange on the muffin halves, adding olive slices for eyeballs, shredded cheese for hair, and green pepper strips for stems.

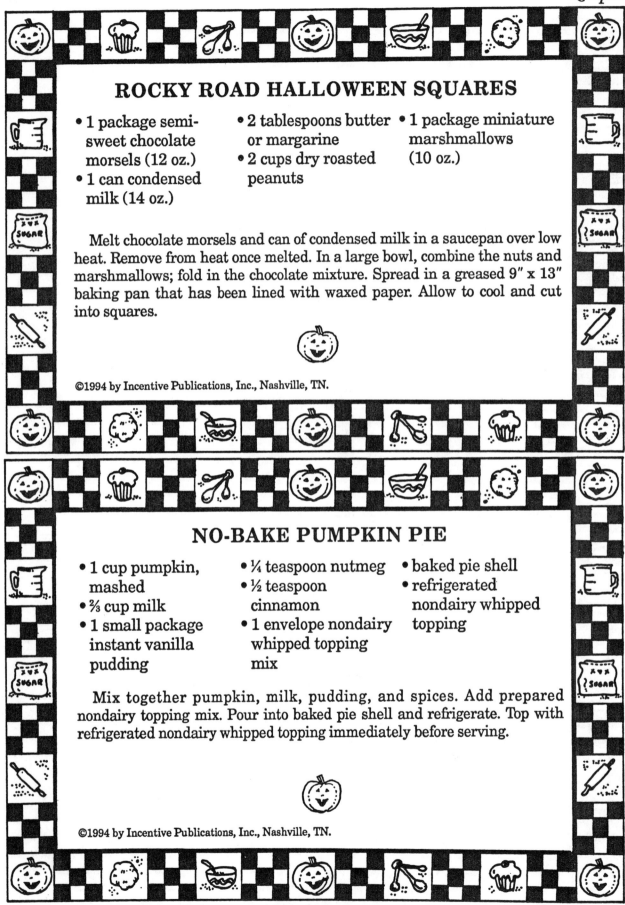

ROCKY ROAD HALLOWEEN SQUARES

- 1 package semi-sweet chocolate morsels (12 oz.)
- 1 can condensed milk (14 oz.)
- 2 tablespoons butter or margarine
- 2 cups dry roasted peanuts
- 1 package miniature marshmallows (10 oz.)

Melt chocolate morsels and can of condensed milk in a saucepan over low heat. Remove from heat once melted. In a large bowl, combine the nuts and marshmallows; fold in the chocolate mixture. Spread in a greased 9" x 13" baking pan that has been lined with waxed paper. Allow to cool and cut into squares.

NO-BAKE PUMPKIN PIE

- 1 cup pumpkin, mashed
- ⅔ cup milk
- 1 small package instant vanilla pudding
- ¼ teaspoon nutmeg
- ½ teaspoon cinnamon
- 1 envelope nondairy whipped topping mix
- baked pie shell
- refrigerated nondairy whipped topping

Mix together pumpkin, milk, pudding, and spices. Add prepared nondairy topping mix. Pour into baked pie shell and refrigerate. Top with refrigerated nondairy whipped topping immediately before serving.

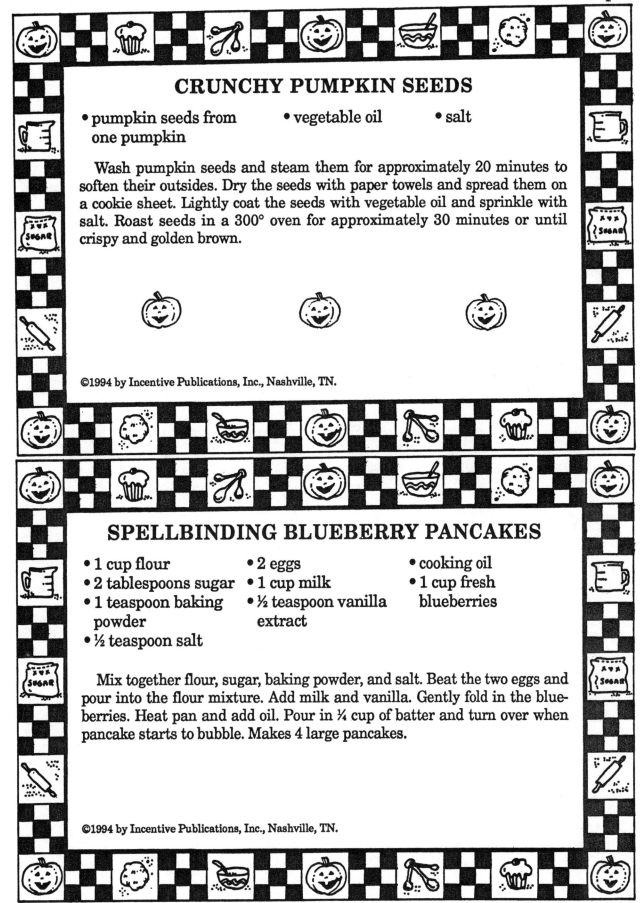

CRUNCHY PUMPKIN SEEDS

- pumpkin seeds from one pumpkin
- vegetable oil
- salt

Wash pumpkin seeds and steam them for approximately 20 minutes to soften their outsides. Dry the seeds with paper towels and spread them on a cookie sheet. Lightly coat the seeds with vegetable oil and sprinkle with salt. Roast seeds in a 300° oven for approximately 30 minutes or until crispy and golden brown.

SPELLBINDING BLUEBERRY PANCAKES

- 1 cup flour
- 2 tablespoons sugar
- 1 teaspoon baking powder
- ½ teaspoon salt
- 2 eggs
- 1 cup milk
- ½ teaspoon vanilla extract
- cooking oil
- 1 cup fresh blueberries

Mix together flour, sugar, baking powder, and salt. Beat the two eggs and pour into the flour mixture. Add milk and vanilla. Gently fold in the blueberries. Heat pan and add oil. Pour in ¼ cup of batter and turn over when pancake starts to bubble. Makes 4 large pancakes.

November

THANKSGIVING

The season of Thanksgiving is a time for appreciating the bounty of the earth. Children delight in learning about the first Thanksgiving: the food, customs, and dress of the Pilgrims make interesting topics of discussion. The following hands-on activities and tempting recipes provide a fun-filled introduction to November's season of sharing.

■ If you have access to antiques, such as a butter churn and butter molds, this is a good time to bring them to the class. Play a guessing game with the children: ask them to guess the uses of various antique objects. You can end the lesson by making **Homemade Butter** and **Cornmeal Bread** (page 30). The butter recipe is quite popular among parents, who frequently call to ask for the instructions.

Making butter is an easy process, and if you add a tablespoon of honey to the butter when it is finished, it tastes even better! The book *Corn is Maize* by Aliki is an excellent choice to read before making the cornbread recipe.

■ A discussion of the Pilgrims and Native Americans can lead to a hat-, apron-, and vest-making session. If you divide your class into two groups of students, the Pilgrims and the Native Americans, each group can make its own special treat for a classroom feast. The Native Americans may decide to cook up some **Indian Slapjacks** (page 31) while the Pilgrims prepare a **Cranberry Relish** (page 31). Before you begin your Thanksgiving feast, however, you can read *The Pilgrims of Plymouth* by Marcia Sewall to give the children an idea of what daily life was like in the Plymouth colony. Also by Sewall is *People of the Breaking Day*, a story which explores the meeting of the Pilgrims and the Indians from the Native American point of view.

■ Ask children to exercise their creative powers by inventing lyrics about the food to be served on Thanksgiving Day. Sing your song to the tune of "The Farmer in the Dell":

> *The turkey ran away, before Thanksgiving Day.*
> *He said, "You'd make a roast of me, so I cannot stay."*
> *The pumpkin ran away, before Thanksgiving Day.*
> *She said, "You'd make a pie of me, so I cannot stay."*
> *The bread ran away, before Thanksgiving Day.*
> *He said, "You'd make a stuffing of me, so I cannot stay."*

The children will create verse after verse if you let them. Often, the more nonsensical the words, the better children like them!

OTHER BOOKS FOR NOVEMBER

Cranberry Thanksgiving by Harry and Wende Devlin.

Little Bear's Thanksgiving by Janice.

Over the River and Through the Woods by Lydia Maria Child.

Story of Jumping Mouse: A Native American Legend by John Steptoe.

Thanksgiving at the Tappleton's by Eileen Spineill.

HOMEMADE BUTTER

- 1 pint whipping cream
- dash of salt

Put whipping cream into a clean glass jar with a tight-fitting lid. Pass the jar around the classroom and have the children shake it while they repeat this chant:

Come, butter, come—come, butter, come.
*Jake is by the garden gate
Waiting for his butter cake.
Come, butter, come—come, butter, come.

* Substitute the name of each child who is shaking the jar.

The butter will be very soft. Drain off excess water before using the butter. Adding a few tablespoons of honey to the butter makes it taste delicious.

©1994 by Incentive Publications, Inc., Nashville, TN.

CORNMEAL BREAD

- ½ cup cornmeal
- ½ cup flour
- 2 tablespoons sugar
- 2 tablespoons baking powder
- ⅓ cup milk
- 1 egg
- 2 tablespoons oil

Preheat oven to 425° and grease muffin tins or a cake pan. In a medium-sized bowl, mix together cornmeal, flour, sugar, and baking powder. Add milk, egg, and oil to the flour mixture and stir until batter is just moistened. Batter should still be lumpy. Pour evenly into muffin tins or cake pan and bake for 15–20 minutes, or until tops are golden brown. (Yield: 6 muffins.)

©1994 by Incentive Publications, Inc., Nashville, TN.

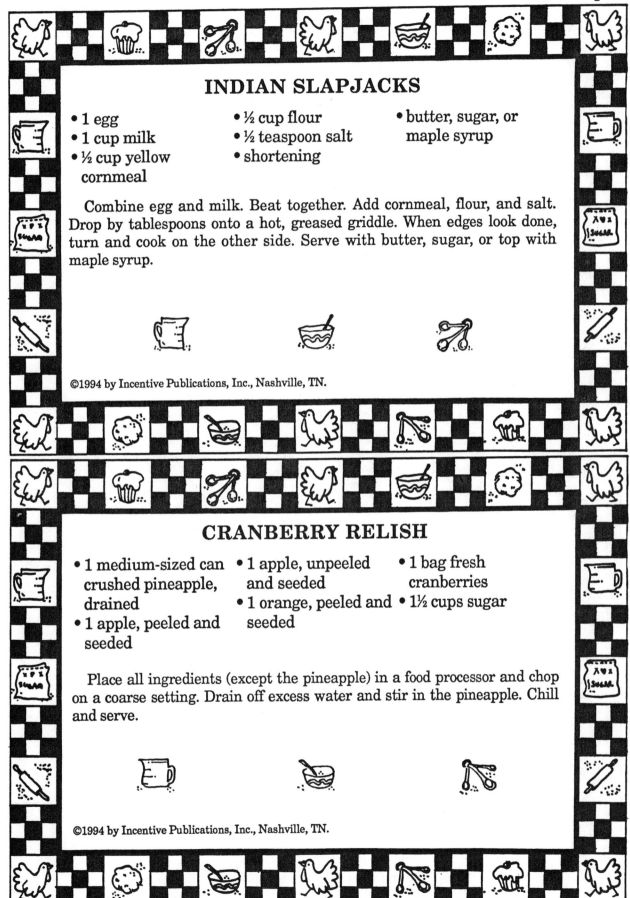

INDIAN SLAPJACKS

- 1 egg
- 1 cup milk
- ½ cup yellow cornmeal
- ½ cup flour
- ½ teaspoon salt
- shortening
- butter, sugar, or maple syrup

Combine egg and milk. Beat together. Add cornmeal, flour, and salt. Drop by tablespoons onto a hot, greased griddle. When edges look done, turn and cook on the other side. Serve with butter, sugar, or top with maple syrup.

CRANBERRY RELISH

- 1 medium-sized can crushed pineapple, drained
- 1 apple, peeled and seeded
- 1 apple, unpeeled and seeded
- 1 orange, peeled and seeded
- 1 bag fresh cranberries
- 1½ cups sugar

Place all ingredients (except the pineapple) in a food processor and chop on a coarse setting. Drain off excess water and stir in the pineapple. Chill and serve.

CRANBERRY PUNCH FOR GRANDMA'S BREAD

- 1 quart cranberry juice
- juice of ½ lemon
- 1 cup orange juice
- 3 cups water
- 1 cup sugar, dissolved
- 1 quart ginger ale

Mix juices and 2 cups water. Dissolve sugar in 1 cup water and stir into the juice mixture. Chill. Just before serving add the ginger ale. Serve with cranberry bread.

BUCKEYES

- ½ cup margarine, melted
- 1 pound powdered sugar
- 1 pound peanut butter
- 2 cups graham crackers, crushed
- 1 teaspoon vanilla extract
- 1 bag chocolate chips, melted

Beat together all of the ingredients except the chocolate chips. Form mixture into walnut-sized ball shapes. Dip these balls halfway into the melted chocolate and place on waxed paper to harden.

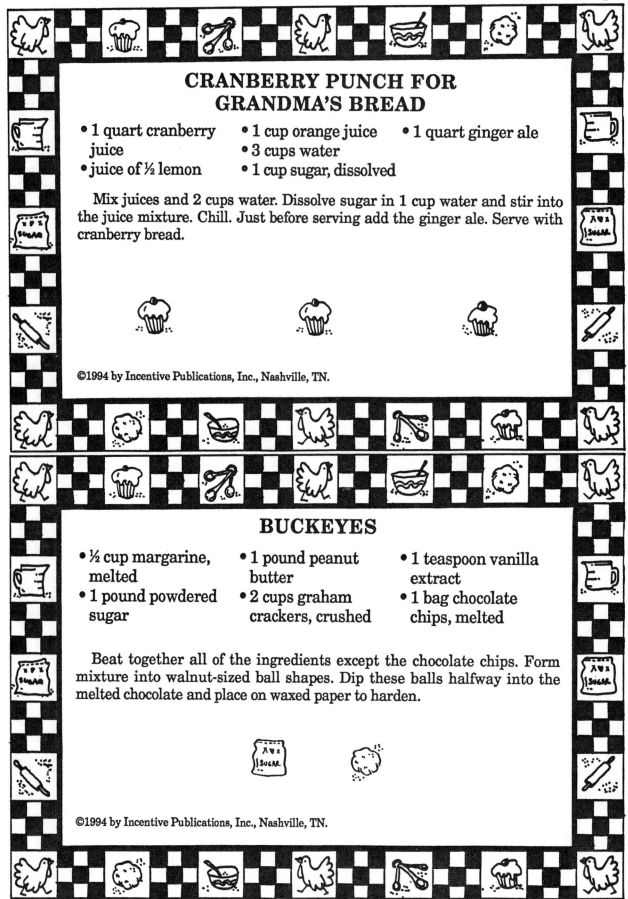

December

CHRISTMAS

Children of all ages enjoy the songs, crafts, and food of the Christmas season. These activities and recipes are guaranteed to add magic to your classroom's festivities.

■ Although many children know the first couple of verses of "Twas the Night Before Christmas" by Clement C. Moore, they often do not know the entire work. Recite the poem to your students and then have them make up their own verses. You may want to begin the new poem with the line: "Twas the week before Christmas, and all through the halls..." Another fun-filled activity has children illustrating each verse of the original poem. Children will have visions of dancing sugarplums in their heads when you make **Sugarplum Treats** (page 36).

■ Teach your students to give homemade gifts to their friends and relatives at this time of year by making **Easy Fudge** and **Pecan Bonbons** (page 37). These treats are easy to make and easy for children to transport home. Most cake decorating stores sell small cardboard boxes which are the perfect size to hold your students' homemade treats. Dr. Seuss's book *How the Grinch Stole Christmas* ties in nicely with a lesson on the importance of giving.

■ A note from each child to Santa and his reindeer can be written directly on the paper plate to be filled with goodies and left out on the night before Christmas. Hand-drawn decorations, **Painted Sugar Cookies** (page 38), and a scoop of mother's oats for Rudolph are perfect treats for the young child to leave out for Santa on Christmas Eve. You might also suggest to parents that it would be nice if Santa wrote a thank-you note on the back of the paper plate. Before this all-important evening, read *The Christmas Santa Almost Missed* by Marian Frances.

CHRISTMAS AROUND THE WORLD

An exploration of Christmas customs from around the world can be as extravagant or as simple as you wish to make it. Discussing Christmas customs, foods, geography, and languages of a variety of countries will increase a child's knowledge of the world. Several different countries can be examined each week, and the children can participate in the learning by making flags and simple traditional crafts each day.

■ The books *Children at Christmastime Around the World* by Satomi Ichikawa, *Christmas Around the World* by Emily Kelley, and *Christmas the World Over* by Daniel J. Foley are full of information about different countries. Children enjoy looking at flags from countries all over the world—you may even want to leave the flags hanging in your room after the Christmas season is over.

■ To end your study of Christmas Around the World, why not host a party to sample foods from the various countries you studied? Parents can be asked to make one dish per household. Some suggested recipes and their accompanying stories include: **Russian Wafers** (page 41), *Babushka: An Old Russian Folktale* by Charles Mikolaycak, and *Ivan: Stories of Old Russia* by Marcus Crouch and Bob Dewar; **Guacamole**

Salad (page 41) and *Nine Days to Christmas: A Story of Mexico* by Marie Hall Ets and Aurora Labastida; **Struter** (page 44) and the story *Christmas in Noisy Village* by Astrid Lindgren; **Apple Charlotte** (page 45) and *Take a Trip to France* by Deborah Newman. Parents and grandparents are usually willing to share recipes and stories of their heritage. Invite them to your classroom to tell stories, explain customs, or cook a favorite recipe.

HANUKKAH

■ There are many books about the potato and its relation to the holiday of Hanukkah. Before you make **Potato Latkes** (page 46) you might want to read one of the following books to your class: *The Chanukkah Guest* by Eric Kimmel, *Hershel and the Hanukkah Goblins* by Eric Kimmel, *I Love Hanukkah: Potato Pancakes All Around* by Marilyn Hirsh, *Latkes and Apple Sauce: A Hanukkah Story* by Fran Manushkin, *Laughing Latkes* by M.B. Goffstein, *The Odd Potato* by Eileen Bluestone Sherman.

■ A discussion of the Dreidel, Menorah, and other Jewish symbols can be found in *A Picture Book of Jewish Holidays* by David Adler. This song about the Dreidel is sung to the tune of "Twinkle, Twinkle Little Star":

> *Dreidel, Dreidel, little top,*
> *Spinning, spinning, 'til you stop.*
> *Landing on the side you choose,*
> *Will I win or will I lose?*
> *Dreidel, Dreidel, little top,*
> *Spinning, spinning, 'til you drop.*

OTHER BOOKS FOR DECEMBER

A Bear for Christmas by Holly Keller.

Christmas Tree Memories by Aliki.

Happy Christmas to All by Ken Compton.

Merry Christmas Strega Nona by Tomie de Paola.

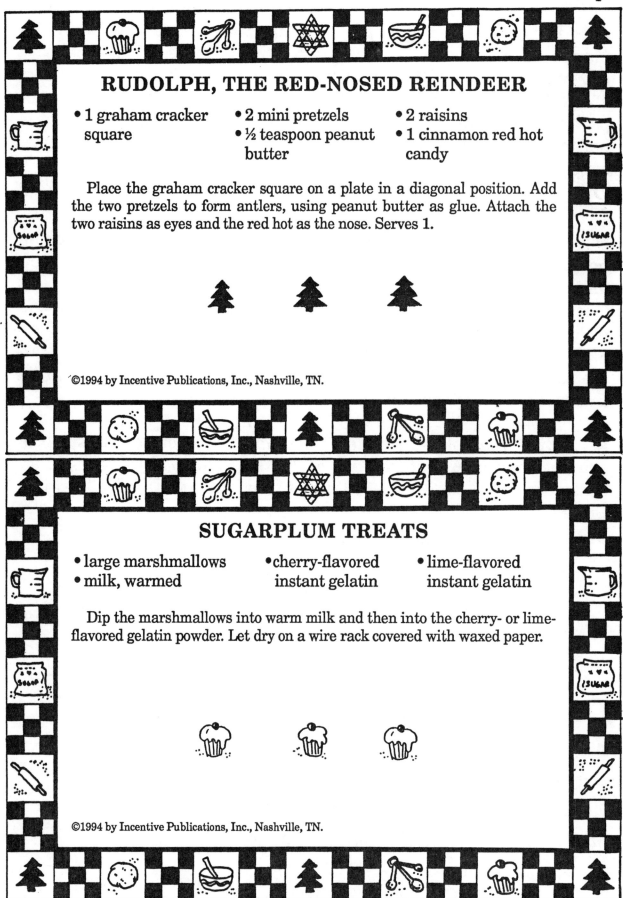

RUDOLPH, THE RED-NOSED REINDEER

- 1 graham cracker square
- 2 mini pretzels
- ½ teaspoon peanut butter
- 2 raisins
- 1 cinnamon red hot candy

Place the graham cracker square on a plate in a diagonal position. Add the two pretzels to form antlers, using peanut butter as glue. Attach the two raisins as eyes and the red hot as the nose. Serves 1.

SUGARPLUM TREATS

- large marshmallows
- milk, warmed
- cherry-flavored instant gelatin
- lime-flavored instant gelatin

Dip the marshmallows into warm milk and then into the cherry- or lime-flavored gelatin powder. Let dry on a wire rack covered with waxed paper.

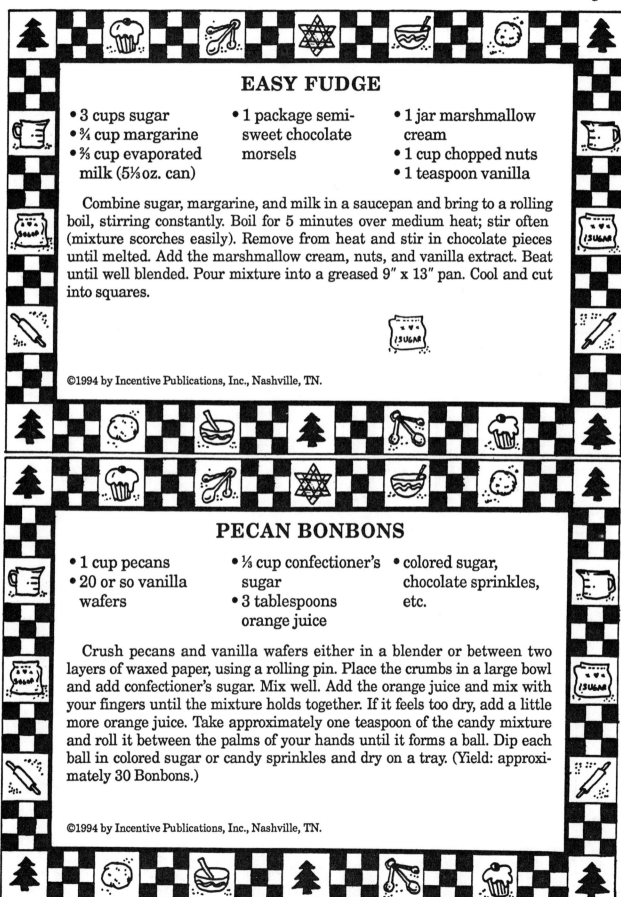

EASY FUDGE

- 3 cups sugar
- ¾ cup margarine
- ⅔ cup evaporated milk (5⅓ oz. can)
- 1 package semi-sweet chocolate morsels
- 1 jar marshmallow cream
- 1 cup chopped nuts
- 1 teaspoon vanilla

Combine sugar, margarine, and milk in a saucepan and bring to a rolling boil, stirring constantly. Boil for 5 minutes over medium heat; stir often (mixture scorches easily). Remove from heat and stir in chocolate pieces until melted. Add the marshmallow cream, nuts, and vanilla extract. Beat until well blended. Pour mixture into a greased 9″ x 13″ pan. Cool and cut into squares.

PECAN BONBONS

- 1 cup pecans
- 20 or so vanilla wafers
- ⅓ cup confectioner's sugar
- 3 tablespoons orange juice
- colored sugar, chocolate sprinkles, etc.

Crush pecans and vanilla wafers either in a blender or between two layers of waxed paper, using a rolling pin. Place the crumbs in a large bowl and add confectioner's sugar. Mix well. Add the orange juice and mix with your fingers until the mixture holds together. If it feels too dry, add a little more orange juice. Take approximately one teaspoon of the candy mixture and roll it between the palms of your hands until it forms a ball. Dip each ball in colored sugar or candy sprinkles and dry on a tray. (Yield: approximately 30 Bonbons.)

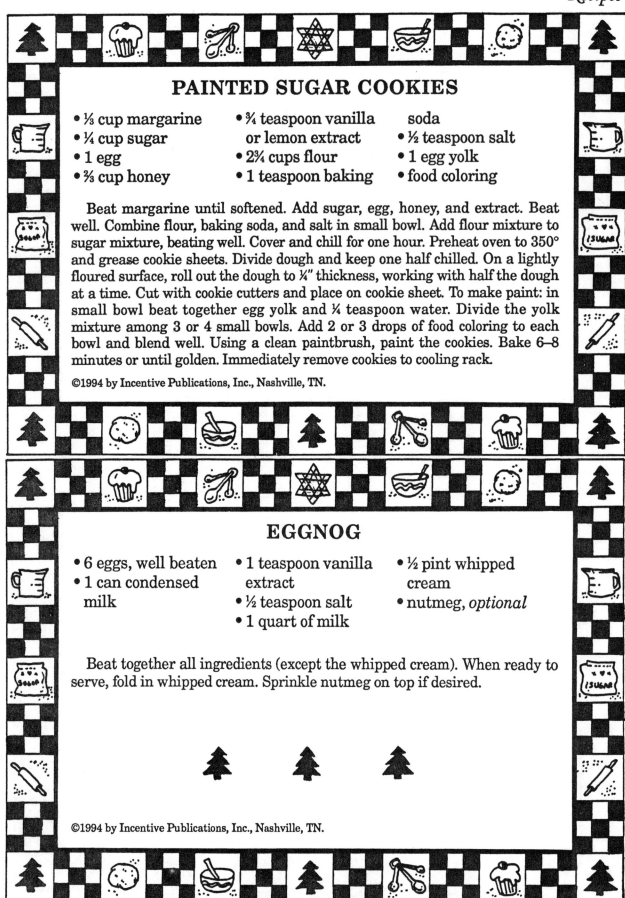

PAINTED SUGAR COOKIES

- ⅓ cup margarine
- ¼ cup sugar
- 1 egg
- ⅔ cup honey
- ¾ teaspoon vanilla or lemon extract
- 2¾ cups flour
- 1 teaspoon baking
- soda
- ½ teaspoon salt
- 1 egg yolk
- food coloring

Beat margarine until softened. Add sugar, egg, honey, and extract. Beat well. Combine flour, baking soda, and salt in small bowl. Add flour mixture to sugar mixture, beating well. Cover and chill for one hour. Preheat oven to 350° and grease cookie sheets. Divide dough and keep one half chilled. On a lightly floured surface, roll out the dough to ¼" thickness, working with half the dough at a time. Cut with cookie cutters and place on cookie sheet. To make paint: in small bowl beat together egg yolk and ¼ teaspoon water. Divide the yolk mixture among 3 or 4 small bowls. Add 2 or 3 drops of food coloring to each bowl and blend well. Using a clean paintbrush, paint the cookies. Bake 6–8 minutes or until golden. Immediately remove cookies to cooling rack.

EGGNOG

- 6 eggs, well beaten
- 1 can condensed milk
- 1 teaspoon vanilla extract
- ½ teaspoon salt
- 1 quart of milk
- ½ pint whipped cream
- nutmeg, *optional*

Beat together all ingredients (except the whipped cream). When ready to serve, fold in whipped cream. Sprinkle nutmeg on top if desired.

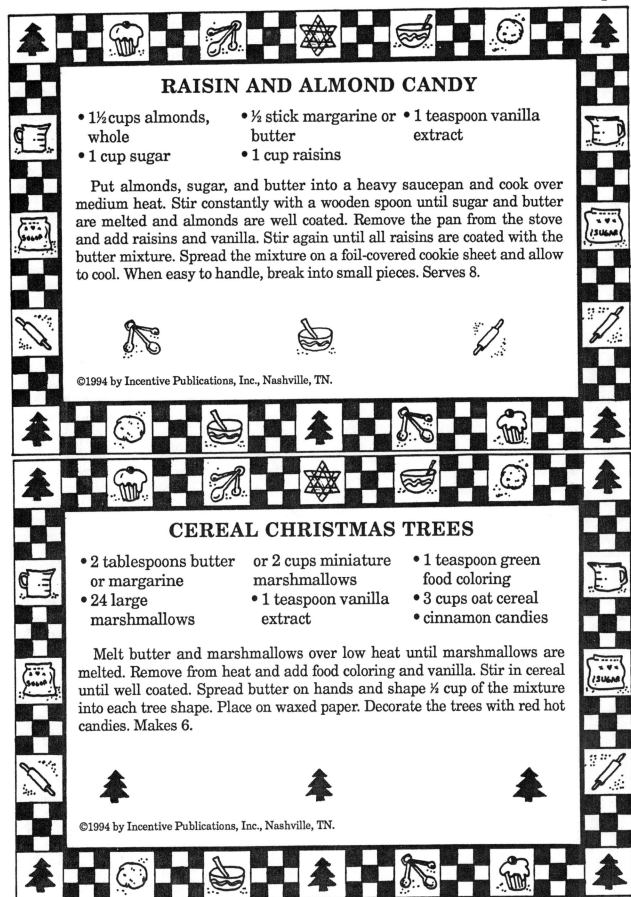

RAISIN AND ALMOND CANDY

- 1½ cups almonds, whole
- 1 cup sugar
- ½ stick margarine or butter
- 1 cup raisins
- 1 teaspoon vanilla extract

Put almonds, sugar, and butter into a heavy saucepan and cook over medium heat. Stir constantly with a wooden spoon until sugar and butter are melted and almonds are well coated. Remove the pan from the stove and add raisins and vanilla. Stir again until all raisins are coated with the butter mixture. Spread the mixture on a foil-covered cookie sheet and allow to cool. When easy to handle, break into small pieces. Serves 8.

CEREAL CHRISTMAS TREES

- 2 tablespoons butter or margarine
- 24 large marshmallows
- or 2 cups miniature marshmallows
- 1 teaspoon vanilla extract
- 1 teaspoon green food coloring
- 3 cups oat cereal
- cinnamon candies

Melt butter and marshmallows over low heat until marshmallows are melted. Remove from heat and add food coloring and vanilla. Stir in cereal until well coated. Spread butter on hands and shape ½ cup of the mixture into each tree shape. Place on waxed paper. Decorate the trees with red hot candies. Makes 6.

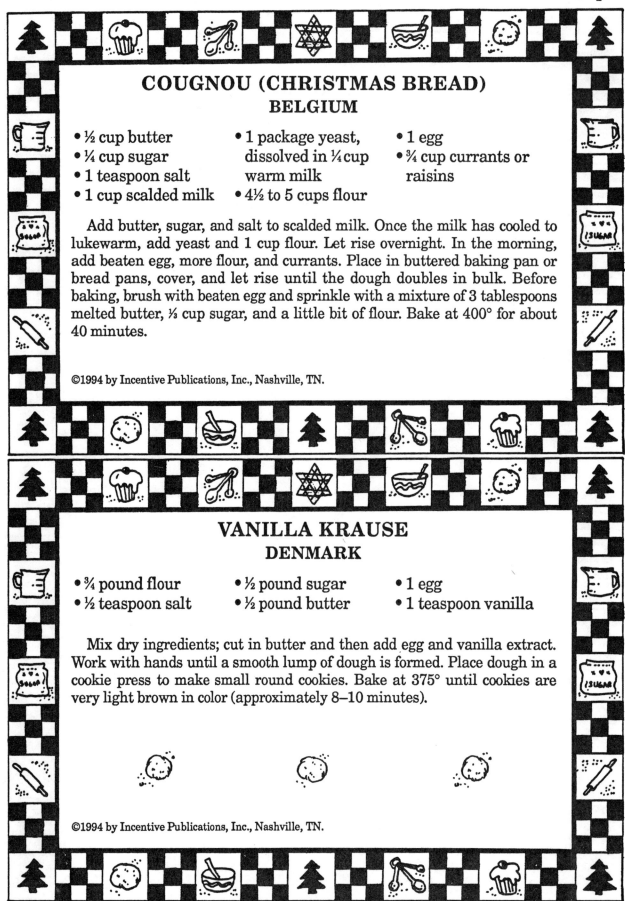

COUGNOU (CHRISTMAS BREAD)
BELGIUM

- ½ cup butter
- ¼ cup sugar
- 1 teaspoon salt
- 1 cup scalded milk
- 1 package yeast, dissolved in ¼ cup warm milk
- 4½ to 5 cups flour
- 1 egg
- ¾ cup currants or raisins

Add butter, sugar, and salt to scalded milk. Once the milk has cooled to lukewarm, add yeast and 1 cup flour. Let rise overnight. In the morning, add beaten egg, more flour, and currants. Place in buttered baking pan or bread pans, cover, and let rise until the dough doubles in bulk. Before baking, brush with beaten egg and sprinkle with a mixture of 3 tablespoons melted butter, ⅓ cup sugar, and a little bit of flour. Bake at 400° for about 40 minutes.

VANILLA KRAUSE
DENMARK

- ¾ pound flour
- ½ teaspoon salt
- ½ pound sugar
- ½ pound butter
- 1 egg
- 1 teaspoon vanilla

Mix dry ingredients; cut in butter and then add egg and vanilla extract. Work with hands until a smooth lump of dough is formed. Place dough in a cookie press to make small round cookies. Bake at 375° until cookies are very light brown in color (approximately 8–10 minutes).

RUSSIAN WAFERS

- 2 cups cake flour, sifted
- 3 teaspoons baking powder
- ½ teaspoon salt
- 1 cup butter
- 1 cup sugar
- 2 eggs, well beaten
- 2 teaspoons vanilla extract
- chopped nuts

Mix together all ingredients, adding flour slowly. Beat until the mixture is very smooth. Chill dough for several hours, or overnight, and then roll it very thin on a floured board, using only a small amount of dough at a time. Cut dough in long thin strips with a well-floured knife and sprinkle each piece with sugar and chopped nuts. Bake at 400° for about 8 minutes. Cool before storing.

GUACAMOLE SALAD
MEXICO

- 2 large ripe avocados
- 1 ripe tomato
- 1 small onion, chopped
- 1 teaspoon lemon juice
- salt and pepper

Peel the avocados and dice into small pieces. Dice the tomato and add it to the avocado mixture. Mix in the chopped onion and lemon juice. Add salt and pepper to taste. Refrigerate. Serve on lettuce leaves, crackers, or with tortilla chips.

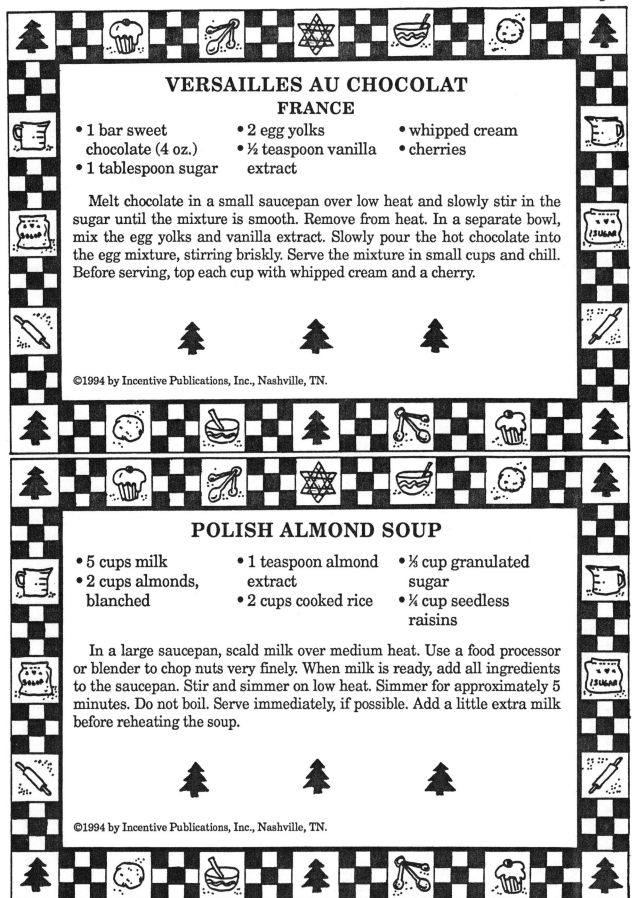

VERSAILLES AU CHOCOLAT
FRANCE

- 1 bar sweet chocolate (4 oz.)
- 1 tablespoon sugar
- 2 egg yolks
- ½ teaspoon vanilla extract
- whipped cream
- cherries

Melt chocolate in a small saucepan over low heat and slowly stir in the sugar until the mixture is smooth. Remove from heat. In a separate bowl, mix the egg yolks and vanilla extract. Slowly pour the hot chocolate into the egg mixture, stirring briskly. Serve the mixture in small cups and chill. Before serving, top each cup with whipped cream and a cherry.

POLISH ALMOND SOUP

- 5 cups milk
- 2 cups almonds, blanched
- 1 teaspoon almond extract
- 2 cups cooked rice
- ⅓ cup granulated sugar
- ¼ cup seedless raisins

In a large saucepan, scald milk over medium heat. Use a food processor or blender to chop nuts very finely. When milk is ready, add all ingredients to the saucepan. Stir and simmer on low heat. Simmer for approximately 5 minutes. Do not boil. Serve immediately, if possible. Add a little extra milk before reheating the soup.

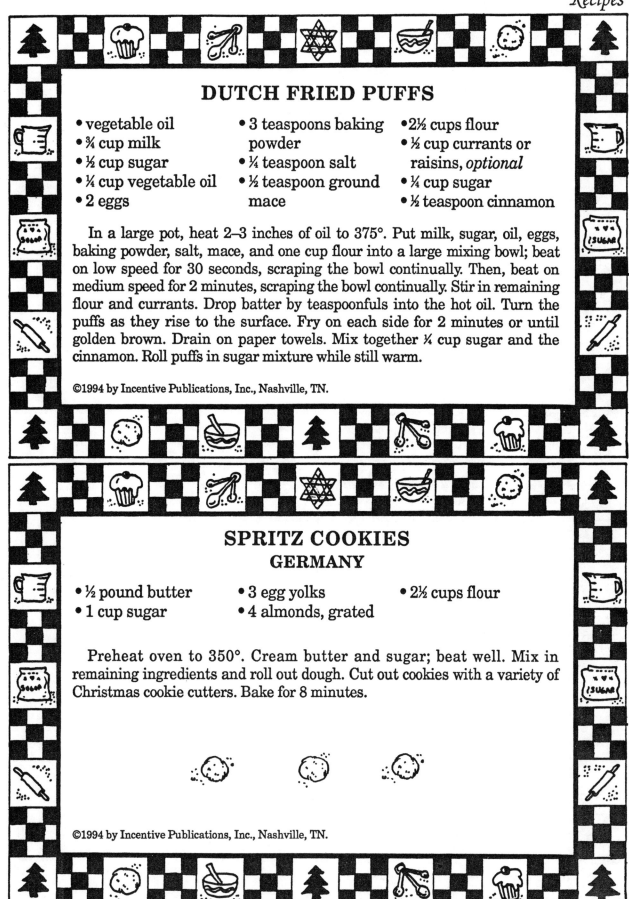

DUTCH FRIED PUFFS

- vegetable oil
- ¾ cup milk
- ½ cup sugar
- ¼ cup vegetable oil
- 2 eggs
- 3 teaspoons baking powder
- ¼ teaspoon salt
- ½ teaspoon ground mace
- 2½ cups flour
- ½ cup currants or raisins, *optional*
- ¼ cup sugar
- ½ teaspoon cinnamon

In a large pot, heat 2–3 inches of oil to 375°. Put milk, sugar, oil, eggs, baking powder, salt, mace, and one cup flour into a large mixing bowl; beat on low speed for 30 seconds, scraping the bowl continually. Then, beat on medium speed for 2 minutes, scraping the bowl continually. Stir in remaining flour and currants. Drop batter by teaspoonfuls into the hot oil. Turn the puffs as they rise to the surface. Fry on each side for 2 minutes or until golden brown. Drain on paper towels. Mix together ¼ cup sugar and the cinnamon. Roll puffs in sugar mixture while still warm.

SPRITZ COOKIES
GERMANY

- ½ pound butter
- 1 cup sugar
- 3 egg yolks
- 4 almonds, grated
- 2½ cups flour

Preheat oven to 350°. Cream butter and sugar; beat well. Mix in remaining ingredients and roll out dough. Cut out cookies with a variety of Christmas cookie cutters. Bake for 8 minutes.

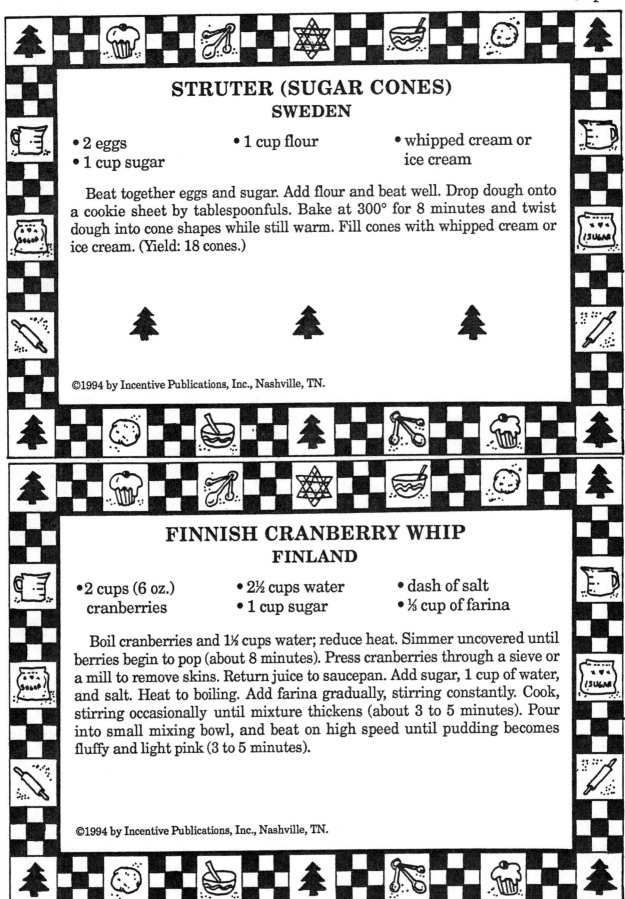

STRUTER (SUGAR CONES)
SWEDEN

- 2 eggs
- 1 cup sugar
- 1 cup flour
- whipped cream or ice cream

Beat together eggs and sugar. Add flour and beat well. Drop dough onto a cookie sheet by tablespoonfuls. Bake at 300° for 8 minutes and twist dough into cone shapes while still warm. Fill cones with whipped cream or ice cream. (Yield: 18 cones.)

FINNISH CRANBERRY WHIP
FINLAND

- 2 cups (6 oz.) cranberries
- 2½ cups water
- 1 cup sugar
- dash of salt
- ⅛ cup of farina

Boil cranberries and 1½ cups water; reduce heat. Simmer uncovered until berries begin to pop (about 8 minutes). Press cranberries through a sieve or a mill to remove skins. Return juice to saucepan. Add sugar, 1 cup of water, and salt. Heat to boiling. Add farina gradually, stirring constantly. Cook, stirring occasionally until mixture thickens (about 3 to 5 minutes). Pour into small mixing bowl, and beat on high speed until pudding becomes fluffy and light pink (3 to 5 minutes).

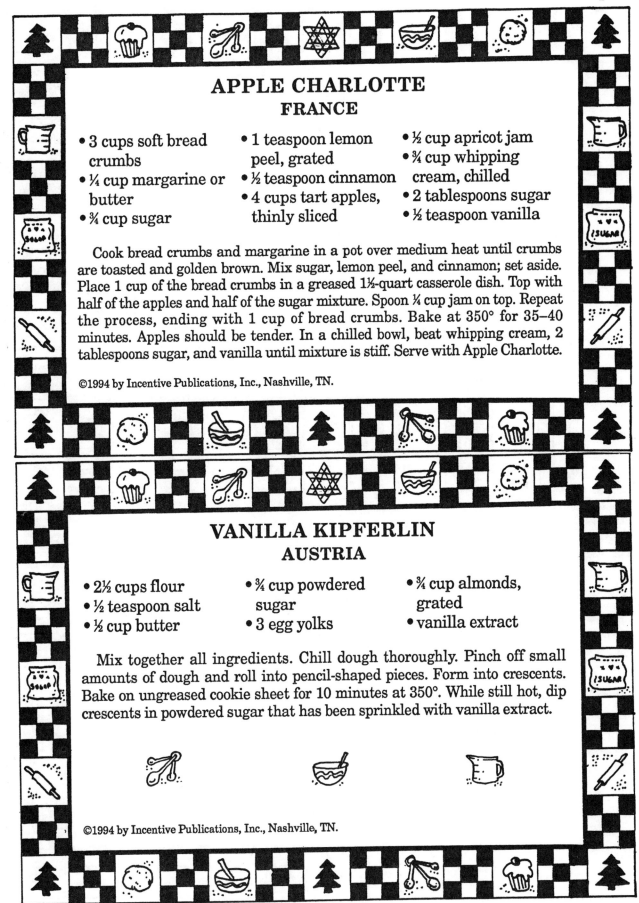

APPLE CHARLOTTE
FRANCE

- 3 cups soft bread crumbs
- ¼ cup margarine or butter
- ¾ cup sugar
- 1 teaspoon lemon peel, grated
- ½ teaspoon cinnamon
- 4 cups tart apples, thinly sliced
- ½ cup apricot jam
- ¾ cup whipping cream, chilled
- 2 tablespoons sugar
- ½ teaspoon vanilla

Cook bread crumbs and margarine in a pot over medium heat until crumbs are toasted and golden brown. Mix sugar, lemon peel, and cinnamon; set aside. Place 1 cup of the bread crumbs in a greased 1½-quart casserole dish. Top with half of the apples and half of the sugar mixture. Spoon ¼ cup jam on top. Repeat the process, ending with 1 cup of bread crumbs. Bake at 350° for 35–40 minutes. Apples should be tender. In a chilled bowl, beat whipping cream, 2 tablespoons sugar, and vanilla until mixture is stiff. Serve with Apple Charlotte.

VANILLA KIPFERLIN
AUSTRIA

- 2½ cups flour
- ½ teaspoon salt
- ½ cup butter
- ¾ cup powdered sugar
- 3 egg yolks
- ¾ cup almonds, grated
- vanilla extract

Mix together all ingredients. Chill dough thoroughly. Pinch off small amounts of dough and roll into pencil-shaped pieces. Form into crescents. Bake on ungreased cookie sheet for 10 minutes at 350°. While still hot, dip crescents in powdered sugar that has been sprinkled with vanilla extract.

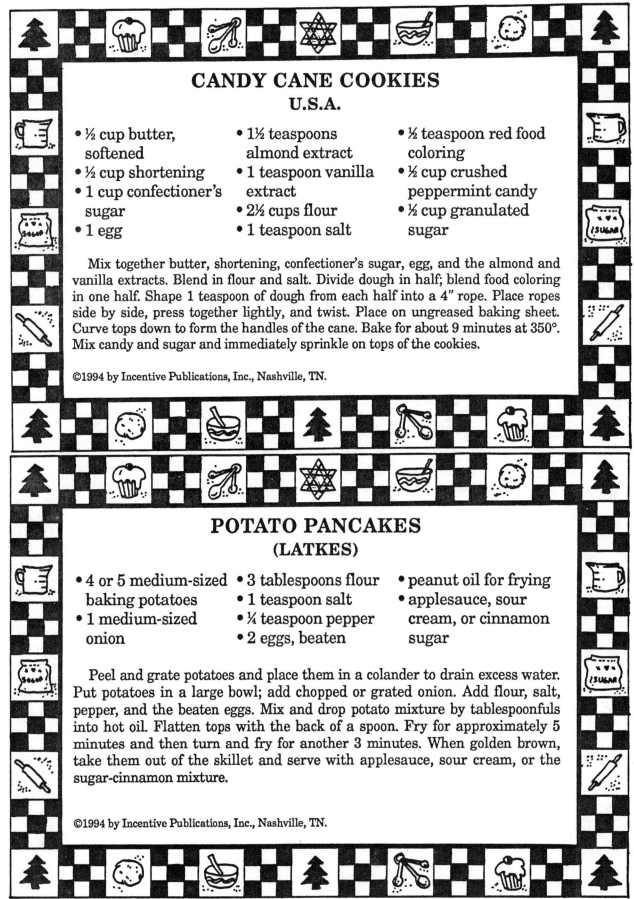

CANDY CANE COOKIES
U.S.A.

- ½ cup butter, softened
- ½ cup shortening
- 1 cup confectioner's sugar
- 1 egg
- 1½ teaspoons almond extract
- 1 teaspoon vanilla extract
- 2½ cups flour
- 1 teaspoon salt
- ½ teaspoon red food coloring
- ½ cup crushed peppermint candy
- ½ cup granulated sugar

Mix together butter, shortening, confectioner's sugar, egg, and the almond and vanilla extracts. Blend in flour and salt. Divide dough in half; blend food coloring in one half. Shape 1 teaspoon of dough from each half into a 4″ rope. Place ropes side by side, press together lightly, and twist. Place on ungreased baking sheet. Curve tops down to form the handles of the cane. Bake for about 9 minutes at 350°. Mix candy and sugar and immediately sprinkle on tops of the cookies.

POTATO PANCAKES
(LATKES)

- 4 or 5 medium-sized baking potatoes
- 1 medium-sized onion
- 3 tablespoons flour
- 1 teaspoon salt
- ¼ teaspoon pepper
- 2 eggs, beaten
- peanut oil for frying
- applesauce, sour cream, or cinnamon sugar

Peel and grate potatoes and place them in a colander to drain excess water. Put potatoes in a large bowl; add chopped or grated onion. Add flour, salt, pepper, and the beaten eggs. Mix and drop potato mixture by tablespoonfuls into hot oil. Flatten tops with the back of a spoon. Fry for approximately 5 minutes and then turn and fry for another 3 minutes. When golden brown, take them out of the skillet and serve with applesauce, sour cream, or the sugar-cinnamon mixture.

January

NEW YEAR'S DAY

■ Discuss what New Year's resolutions are and why people make them. What kinds of resolutions could the students make as a class? Read *New Year's Day* by Lynn Groh and discuss traditional symbols of the new year.

■ People often wish each other good fortune at the start of a new year. Pose the question: "If you were responsible for writing the fortunes found inside fortune cookies, what would you write?" Have the students write fortunes to be placed inside **Fortune Cookies** (page 49).

CHINESE NEW YEAR

According to the Chinese lunar calendar, the new year begins on the second new moon after the first day of winter. This day falls in late January or early February.

■ Read Emily Kelley's *Happy New Year*, which contains a discussion of New Year traditions from China and other countries around the world and make **Chinese Egg Rice Soup** (page 50).

MARTIN LUTHER KING, JR., DAY

The month of January provides the opportunity to examine one of the United States of America's great leaders: Dr. Martin Luther King, Jr. Dr. King, born on January 15, 1929, had a dream that all people of all colors and beliefs would one day live in harmony with each other.

■ Discuss Dr. King's dream with your students. Ask them what kinds of dreams they have. *A Picture Book of Martin Luther King, Jr.*, by David Adler is a nice book to read aloud to students before discussing his life.

■ Sharing the concept of the importance of individuality is a crucial lesson for young children to learn. Making **Friendship Stew** (page 50) will help to symbolize and reinforce this notion.

A. A. MILNE'S BIRTHDAY

The birthday of A. A. Milne (January 18, 1882), the author of the lovable Winnie-the-Pooh stories, provides an excellent reason to study various bears in literature.

■ Compare and contrast the bears in *Winnie-the-Pooh*, "Goldilocks and the Three Bears," *Paddington Bear* by Michael Bond, and *Corduroy* by Don Freeman. Similarities and differences in size, color, clothing, and places of residence can be noted and discussed. **Honeybees** (page 51), **A Bear's Honey-Bread Pudding** (page 51), or an oatmeal porridge would serve well as the food of the day.

OTHER BOOKS FOR JANUARY

Arthur's Honey Bear by Lillian Hoban.
The Big Book for Peace edited by Ann Durrell and Marilyn Sachs.
The Black Snowman by Phil Mendez.
Happy Birthday Moon by Frank Asch.
Small Bear's Busy Day by Adelaide Holl.
We're Going on a Bear Hunt by Michael Rosen.

NEW YEAR'S PRETZELS

- 1 package active dry yeast
- 1½ cups warm water
- 1 tablespoon sugar
- 1 egg, beaten
- 3–4 cups flour
- 1 tablespoon coarse salt

Preheat oven to 375°. Combine yeast, warm water, and sugar in a small bowl. Let stand a minute and then stir to dissolve yeast and sugar. Add egg and mix; then add 3 cups of flour and the salt. Knead dough and add remaining cup of flour, if needed. Continue to knead dough until it becomes smooth and stretchy. Pinch off a piece of dough the size of a golf ball and roll it between your hands to form a rope. Shape into a pretzel. Place on a greased cookie sheet and sprinkle with coarse salt. Bake for 12–15 minutes.

FORTUNE COOKIES

- ¼ cup flour
- 2 tablespoons brown sugar
- 1 tablespoon cornstarch
- dash of salt
- 2 tablespoons cooking oil
- 1 egg white, stiffly beaten
- ¼ teaspoon vanilla or lemon flavoring
- 3 tablespoons water
- 8–10 fortunes, typed on paper strips

Combine flour, sugar, cornstarch, and salt. Stir in oil and fold in egg white until mixture is smooth. Add flavoring and water; mix well. In a small skillet pour one tablespoon of batter, spreading it to a 3″ circle. Cook over medium heat for 4 minutes or until lightly browned. Turn with a spatula and cook one more minute. Remove from skillet and quickly place a fortune paper in the center of the cookie's circle. Fold cookie in half over the edge of a glass and then in half again. Hold for a few seconds until cool, and then place in an empty egg carton to help cookie hold its shape. If cookies aren't crisp enough, toast them in the oven at 300° for 10 minutes.

CHINESE EGG RICE SOUP

- 6 cups chicken broth
- 2 eggs, beaten
- 2 cups cooked rice

Place the broth in a saucepan and bring to a boil. Pour in the beaten eggs in a slow, steady stream. Stir. Let eggs and broth cook for about 2 minutes. Stir in the cooked rice until warmed throughout. Serves 12.

FRIENDSHIP STEW

- 1 stalk celery
- 1 green pepper
- 1 tomato
- 1 medium-sized onion
- green peas
- 1 zucchini
- green beans
- 1 head cabbage
- 6 cups water
- 2 cups tomato puree
- 3 tablespoons chicken stock

Ask each child to bring from home one or more of the vegetables needed for the stew. Children wash and dice the vegetables and then add the vegetables, water, tomato puree, and chicken stock to a large pot. Bring stew to a boil; lower heat and simmer for 30 minutes.

HONEYBEES

- ½ cup peanut butter
- 1 tablespoon honey
- ⅓ cup nonfat dry milk powder
- 2 tablespoons sesame seeds
- 2 tablespoons toasted wheat germ
- unsweetened cocoa powder
- sliced almonds

Combine peanut butter and honey in a bowl and mix well. Stir in dry milk powder, sesame seeds, and wheat germ until well blended. Shape by teaspoonfuls into ovals to resemble bees. Place on a cookie sheet covered with waxed paper. Dip a toothpick into the cocoa powder and press the toothpick gently across the tops of bees to make 3 stripes on each. Place almonds on the sides of each to represent the bee's wings. Chill for 30 minutes. (Yield: 28–30 Honeybees.)

©1994 by Incentive Publications, Inc., Nashville, TN.

A BEAR'S HONEY–BREAD PUDDING

- 1 egg
- 2 teaspoons honey
- ½ teaspoon vanilla extract
- ¾ cup milk
- 1 slice bread
- cinnamon, to taste

Preheat oven to 350°. Place egg in a small glass baking dish and beat with a fork until well mixed. Add honey and vanilla to egg, mixing well. Beat in milk. Tear bread into 8 pieces. Place in egg mixture, pressing with a fork to cover well. Soak for several minutes and sprinkle with cinnamon. Bake for 25–30 minutes or until set. Makes 1 serving.

©1994 by Incentive Publications, Inc., Nashville, TN.

February

GROUNDHOG DAY

According to legend, the groundhog emerges from hibernation on February 2nd. If he sees his shadow, there will be six more weeks of winter. If he does not see his shadow, spring will arrive early.

■   Take a trip outside to play a game of "Try To Step on My Shadow." This game is played like "Tag," with the exception that in order to tag someone out of the game, the person who is "It" must step on another player's shadow.

■   Project light on a curtain or a blank wall and have fun making shadows. Children can practice making dogs, bunnies, fish, and other shadowy creatures.

■ Read Sharon Shebar's *Ground Hog Day* and cook up a mess of **Dirt Dessert** (page 56).

■ Children have fun pretending to be groundhogs while nibbling on Groundhog Food (a variety of raw vegetables). Help the children clean and slice their assorted raw vegetables for a snack. One child can pretend to be a groundhog while his or her partner acts like the groundhog's shadow, trying to do everything the groundhog does. A good book to accompany this activity is *Nature's Children: Woodchucks* by Laime Dingwall.

ABRAHAM LINCOLN'S BIRTHDAY

Abraham Lincoln, the 16th President of the United States of America, was born on February 12, 1809.

■ Ask your students to close their eyes and hold out their hands flat, and tell them that you are going to give each one his or her own picture of Abraham Lincoln. Place a penny in each child's hand. Provide a magnifying glass to enable the students to closely examine their pennies. Point out the tiny statue of Lincoln inside his memorial on the back of the penny.

■ After reading *If You Grew Up with Abraham Lincoln* by Ann McGovern, you might bring to class an oil lamp. Light the lamp and turn off all of the lights to show students what it is like without the benefit of electric lights, as it was when Abraham Lincoln was a boy. Students enjoy drawing pictures or listening to a story without the aid of electric lights.

■ Old-fashioned **Johnnycakes** (page 57), much like what Abraham Lincoln might have carried with him while traveling to school, can add a fun-filled dimension to learning about the life and times of the 16th President of the United States. Other interesting books on Lincoln are *Abraham Lincoln* by Patricia Miles Martin or *Abe Lincoln, The Young Years* by Keith Brandt.

VALENTINE'S DAY

February is the perfect month to begin a lesson on the human heart. For young children, studying the heart should be kept simple. For example, you may want to introduce only the size and shape of the heart, as well as ways to keep a heart healthy.

■ Each student can cut from construction paper three heart shapes, one slightly larger than the other two. Help each student write the words "Heart Smart" on his or her biggest heart. On the two smaller hearts, help each write examples of how to maintain a healthy heart. Some examples include, "Don't Smoke," "Get Plenty Of Exercise," "Drink Milk," "Eat Your Vegetables," etc. Have the students brainstorm to come up with their own ideas. After the hearts are finished, make a mobile by hanging the two smaller hearts from the larger one. An appropriate accompanying story is *Hear Your Heart* by Paul Showers. It is also a good idea to invite the school nurse to your classroom to serve as a resource person when discussing the human heart.

■ After a lesson on the heart, make healthy and delicious **Heart Sandwiches** (page 58).

■ Children will have fun reading the story of *The Missing Tarts* by B.G. Hennessy and then baking some tasty **Heart Tarts** (page 58).

GEORGE WASHINGTON'S BIRTHDAY

George Washington, the first President of the United States, was born on February 22, 1732. His nickname is the "Father of His Country."

■ A history lesson about the first President of the United States, including a discussion of the tale of the cherry tree, can be accompanied by making **Cherry Delight** (page 60). While the tarts are chilling, the children might enjoy making their own versions of a cherry tree. To make a tree, cut the leaves from green construction paper, the tree trunk from brown construction paper, and the cherries from red construction paper. Once constructed, the tree should be cut in half and put back together with a paper fastener so that it can stand upright or bend in half. Your students will have fun toppling their trees as they pretend to be George Washington chopping down the cherry tree.

■ Martha and Charles Shapp's book *Let's Find Out About George Washington* will help young students discover more about the Father of the United States of America.

OTHER BOOKS FOR FEBRUARY

Four Valentines in a Rainstorm by Felicia Bond.

Valentine Bears by Eve Bunting.

Valentine's Day Grump by Rose Greydanus.

DIRT DESSERT

- 2 packages cream cheese, softened
- 2 cups powdered sugar
- 1 large container refrigerated whipped topping
- 1 large box vanilla instant pudding
- 3 cups milk
- 1 teaspoon vanilla extract
- 1 package chocolate sandwich cookies, crushed with the middles removed
- 1 paper groundhog

Mix cream cheese and powdered sugar. Add to whipped topping. Combine the vanilla pudding mix and milk and add to cream cheese mixture; stir until mixture thickens. Place in a clean flower pot and top with crushed chocolate cookies to represent dirt. Serve with paper groundhog peeking from the "dirt."

GROUNDHOG SUNDAES

- 1 quart vanilla ice cream, cut in slices
- chocolate sandwich cookies
- chocolate sauce

Place a slice of ice cream topped with a cookie on each plate. Drizzle chocolate sauce across the ice cream and onto the plate to suggest a shadow.

CHEESE LOG

- 1 package cream cheese (8 oz.)
- 1 small jar blue cheese spread
- 1 small jar pineapple cheese spread
- 1 cup nuts, ground
- 1 box party crackers

Mix the cream cheese with the cheese spreads. Chill the mixture for 15 minutes. Place a plastic bag on each of your hands and mold the cheese into a log shape. Place the log on a small platter and chill for 2 hours. Pat crushed nuts on the outside of the log before serving. Eat with party crackers.

JOHNNYCAKES (TRAVELIN' BREAD)

- 1 cup cornmeal, yellow or white
- ¾ teaspoon salt
- 2 teaspoons sugar
- 1 cup water
- 2 tablespoons butter
- ¼ cup milk
- butter, margarine, or oil for frying
- maple syrup

Mix cornmeal, salt, and sugar in a medium-sized bowl. Measure water and the 2 tablespoons butter into a medium saucepan and heat to a rolling boil. Immediately pour hot mixture over the cornmeal mixture in a slow trickle, stirring constantly. When butter is melted and all liquid is absorbed, add milk. Mixture should be fairly thick. Heat griddle or skillet and add butter or oil. When butter or oil sizzles, drop johnnycake batter from a large tablespoon onto skillet, forming cakes that are about 4" in diameter. When golden brown on the underside, lift carefully and turn to the other side. Serve with maple syrup. (Yield: 12 Johnnycakes.)

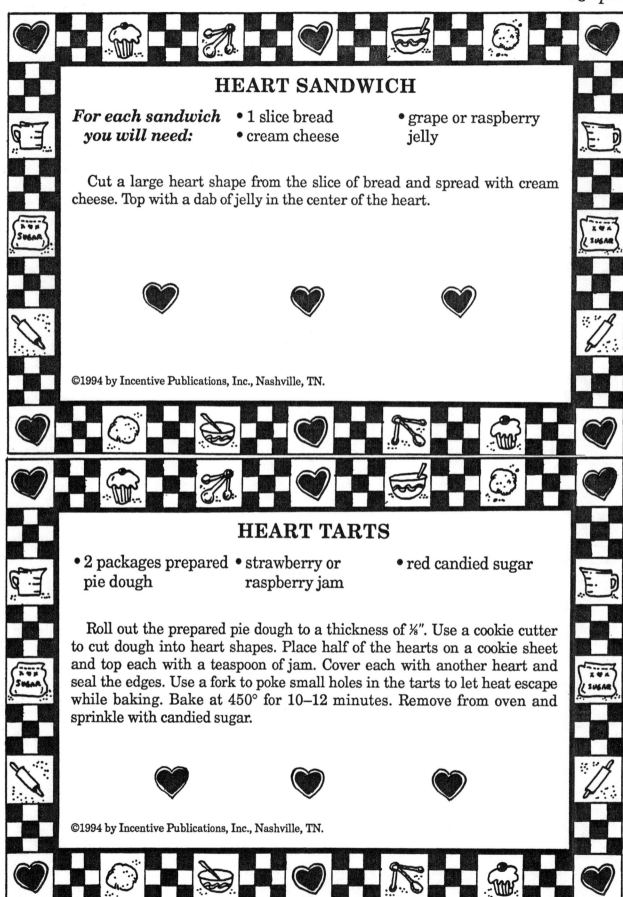

HEART SANDWICH

***For each sandwich
you will need:***
- 1 slice bread
- cream cheese
- grape or raspberry jelly

Cut a large heart shape from the slice of bread and spread with cream cheese. Top with a dab of jelly in the center of the heart.

HEART TARTS

- 2 packages prepared pie dough
- strawberry or raspberry jam
- red candied sugar

Roll out the prepared pie dough to a thickness of ⅛". Use a cookie cutter to cut dough into heart shapes. Place half of the hearts on a cookie sheet and top each with a teaspoon of jam. Cover each with another heart and seal the edges. Use a fork to poke small holes in the tarts to let heat escape while baking. Bake at 450° for 10–12 minutes. Remove from oven and sprinkle with candied sugar.

PINK PUNCH

- 1 small package raspberry gelatin
- 1 cup boiling water
- 1 can frozen red punch (6 oz.)
- 3 cups cold water
- 1 quart ginger ale
- 1 quart raspberry sherbet
- ½ pint fresh raspberries, *optional*

Mix gelatin with boiling water and stir until gelatin dissolves. Pour into a large punch bowl and add frozen punch. Stir. Add cold water and chill. 15 minutes before serving, stir in ginger ale. Float scoops of sherbet in punch bowl. Add several raspberries to each cup as punch is served. (Yield: 15 servings.)

PARTY COOKIES OR DOUGHNUTS

- 2 dozen sugar cookies or plain cake doughnuts
- pink icing
- red icing
- white icing
- assorted pink and red candy decorations

Children decorate the cookies or doughnuts to their own tastes using the colored icing, sugar, and decorations.

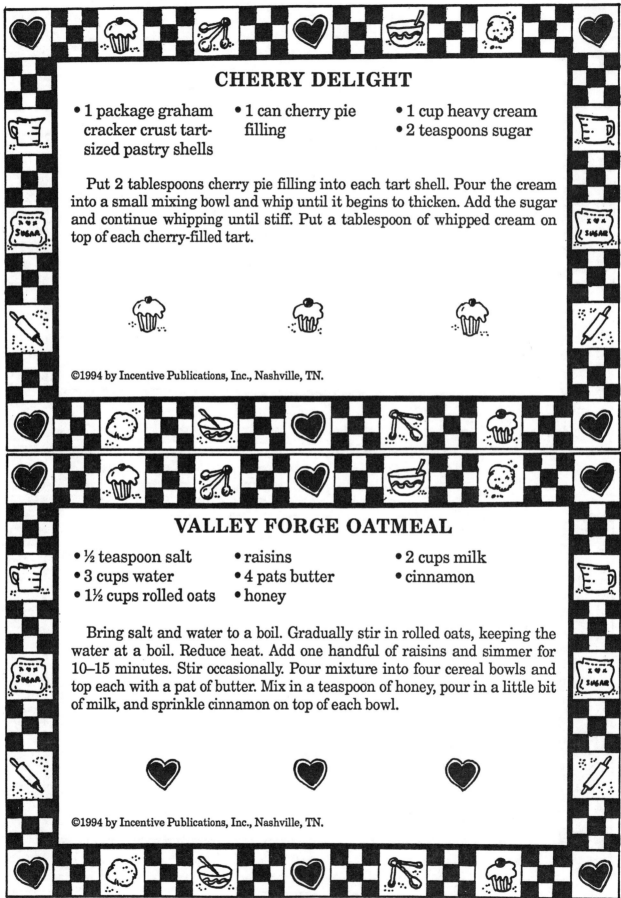

CHERRY DELIGHT

- 1 package graham cracker crust tart-sized pastry shells
- 1 can cherry pie filling
- 1 cup heavy cream
- 2 teaspoons sugar

Put 2 tablespoons cherry pie filling into each tart shell. Pour the cream into a small mixing bowl and whip until it begins to thicken. Add the sugar and continue whipping until stiff. Put a tablespoon of whipped cream on top of each cherry-filled tart.

VALLEY FORGE OATMEAL

- ½ teaspoon salt
- 3 cups water
- 1½ cups rolled oats
- raisins
- 4 pats butter
- honey
- 2 cups milk
- cinnamon

Bring salt and water to a boil. Gradually stir in rolled oats, keeping the water at a boil. Reduce heat. Add one handful of raisins and simmer for 10–15 minutes. Stir occasionally. Pour mixture into four cereal bowls and top each with a pat of butter. Mix in a teaspoon of honey, pour in a little bit of milk, and sprinkle cinnamon on top of each bowl.

March

ST. PATRICK'S DAY

March 17 is a feast day celebrating the work of Saint Patrick, a bishop who converted many Irish people to Christianity during the early 5th century.

■ Children love to participate in treasure hunts. On St. Patrick's Day, organize a hunt for the Leprechaun's lost pot of gold. Seal a handful of candy coins (enough for the entire class) in a plastic bag and place in a black pot. Hide the pot somewhere on school grounds. Write clues for locating the pot on the blackboard and help children read them. One might read:

> *I'm a tricky little fellow, so clever and green;*
> *I love to play tricks and keep from being seen.*
> *I've left you a treasure: a pot full of gold.*
> *Why not look where the lunches are sold?*

When the children reach the cafeteria, they might find another clue that reads:

> *My clever, dear children, how quickly you have sped.*
> *Now go and look for a shamrock that is red.*

Make sure you hide the red shamrock somewhere visible and in a familiar place. When the children find it, the last clue could read:

> *This is the last clue, and it's just what you need.*
> *So walk quietly to the room where you read.*

After the children have located the treasure in the library, make arrangements with the librarian to read aloud to the children *Clever Tom and the Leprechaun* by Linda Shute. Later that day (or on another day), cook **Irish Potato Candy** (page 63) or **Leprechaun Leaps** (page 63) to celebrate a bit o' the green.

SPRING

The first day of spring is March 21st.

■ Have students help decorate the classroom bulletin board. You may want to write on the bulletin board the slogan "Spring Is In The Air" and let children add construction paper birds, kites, bees, clouds, nests, and flowers.

■ Discuss with students some of the signs of springtime after reading the book *First Comes Spring* by Anne F. Rockwell. End your week-long examination of spring by making **Bird Nests** (page 65).

OTHER BOOKS FOR MARCH

Daniel O'Rourk by Gerald McDermott.

The Search for Spring by Moira Miller.

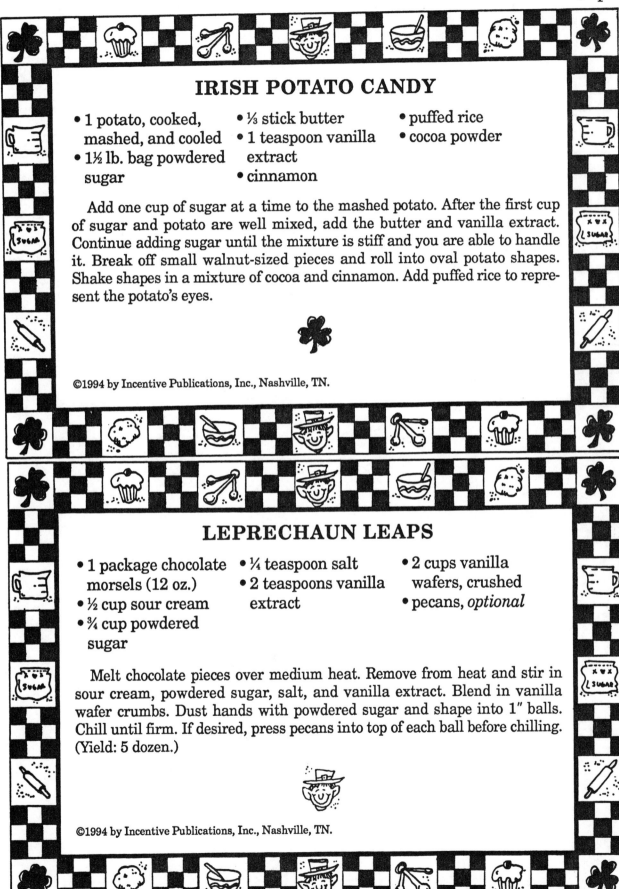

IRISH POTATO CANDY

- 1 potato, cooked, mashed, and cooled
- 1½ lb. bag powdered sugar
- ⅓ stick butter
- 1 teaspoon vanilla extract
- cinnamon
- puffed rice
- cocoa powder

Add one cup of sugar at a time to the mashed potato. After the first cup of sugar and potato are well mixed, add the butter and vanilla extract. Continue adding sugar until the mixture is stiff and you are able to handle it. Break off small walnut-sized pieces and roll into oval potato shapes. Shake shapes in a mixture of cocoa and cinnamon. Add puffed rice to represent the potato's eyes.

LEPRECHAUN LEAPS

- 1 package chocolate morsels (12 oz.)
- ½ cup sour cream
- ¾ cup powdered sugar
- ¼ teaspoon salt
- 2 teaspoons vanilla extract
- 2 cups vanilla wafers, crushed
- pecans, *optional*

Melt chocolate pieces over medium heat. Remove from heat and stir in sour cream, powdered sugar, salt, and vanilla extract. Blend in vanilla wafer crumbs. Dust hands with powdered sugar and shape into 1" balls. Chill until firm. If desired, press pecans into top of each ball before chilling. (Yield: 5 dozen.)

GREEN SPAGHETTI

- 8 ounces fresh spinach
- ¾ cup olive oil
- ¼ cup parsley, coarsely chopped
- ¼ cup Parmesan cheese
- 2 teaspoons dried basil
- ½ teaspoon pepper
- 1 clove garlic, minced
- 12 oz. thin spaghetti

Wash spinach and chop coarsely. Place olive oil in blender and add spinach, parsley, cheese, basil, pepper, and garlic, processing after each additional ingredient has been added until mixture is smooth. Cook spaghetti and drain. Spoon pasta onto serving plates and top with green sauce. Serves 4.

SPINACH SALAD

Salad:
- spinach
- sprouts
- mushrooms
- onions
- bacon bits
- croutons

Dressing:
- ½ cup salad oil
- ⅓ cup catsup
- ⅓ cup sugar
- 1 tablespoon Worcestershire sauce

Toss salad ingredients and mix dressing ingredients well. Pour dressing onto salad greens and serve.

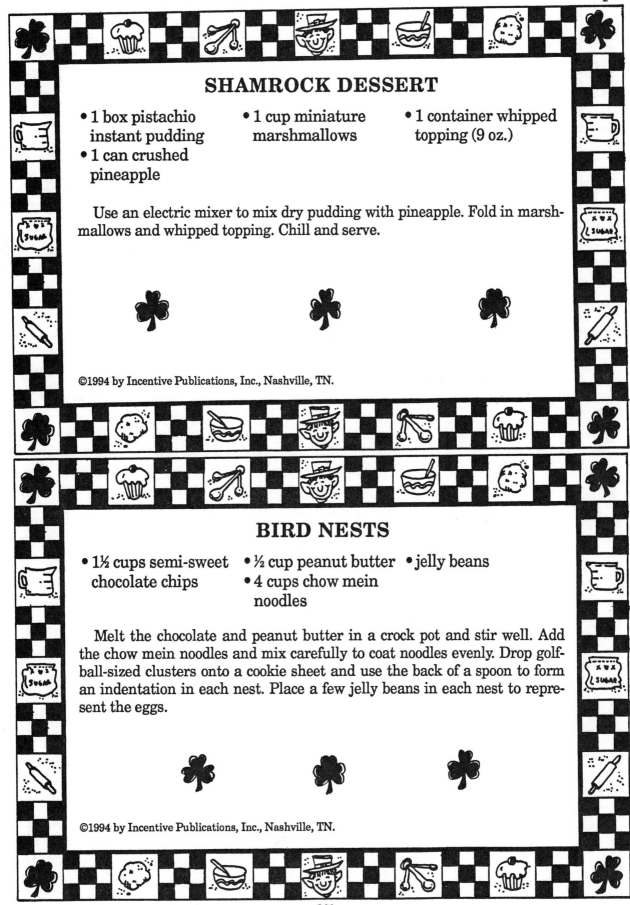

SHAMROCK DESSERT

- 1 box pistachio instant pudding
- 1 can crushed pineapple
- 1 cup miniature marshmallows
- 1 container whipped topping (9 oz.)

Use an electric mixer to mix dry pudding with pineapple. Fold in marshmallows and whipped topping. Chill and serve.

BIRD NESTS

- 1½ cups semi-sweet chocolate chips
- ½ cup peanut butter
- 4 cups chow mein noodles
- jelly beans

Melt the chocolate and peanut butter in a crock pot and stir well. Add the chow mein noodles and mix carefully to coat noodles evenly. Drop golf-ball-sized clusters onto a cookie sheet and use the back of a spoon to form an indentation in each nest. Place a few jelly beans in each nest to represent the eggs.

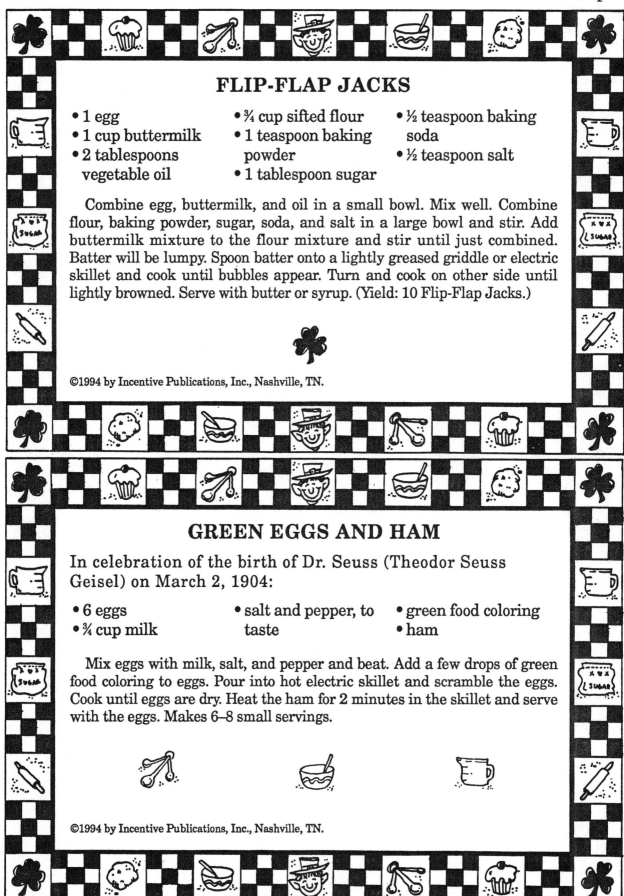

FLIP-FLAP JACKS

- 1 egg
- 1 cup buttermilk
- 2 tablespoons vegetable oil
- ¾ cup sifted flour
- 1 teaspoon baking powder
- 1 tablespoon sugar
- ½ teaspoon baking soda
- ½ teaspoon salt

Combine egg, buttermilk, and oil in a small bowl. Mix well. Combine flour, baking powder, sugar, soda, and salt in a large bowl and stir. Add buttermilk mixture to the flour mixture and stir until just combined. Batter will be lumpy. Spoon batter onto a lightly greased griddle or electric skillet and cook until bubbles appear. Turn and cook on other side until lightly browned. Serve with butter or syrup. (Yield: 10 Flip-Flap Jacks.)

GREEN EGGS AND HAM

In celebration of the birth of Dr. Seuss (Theodor Seuss Geisel) on March 2, 1904:

- 6 eggs
- ¾ cup milk
- salt and pepper, to taste
- green food coloring
- ham

Mix eggs with milk, salt, and pepper and beat. Add a few drops of green food coloring to eggs. Pour into hot electric skillet and scramble the eggs. Cook until eggs are dry. Heat the ham for 2 minutes in the skillet and serve with the eggs. Makes 6–8 small servings.

April

APRIL FOOL'S DAY

■ Plan a crazy, mixed-up day for the first of April. Send a note home to parents ahead of time to tell them you are going to celebrate April Fool's Day by having the children come to school dressed incorrectly (e.g., wearing differently colored socks, unmatched shoes, hats on backwards, one pant leg rolled up and the other rolled down, etc.). When children arrive at school, let each one stand up and have the others guess what is inappropriate about his or her attire. You might even try to mix up some items in the room and see if students can guess which ones are out of place.

■ *Five Silly Fisherman* by Roberta Edwards, *Foolish Giant* by Bruce and Katherine Coville, or *April Fool's* by Fernando Krahn are perfect

books to read after a day of foolishness. Don't forget to serve an **Inside-Out Snack** (page 69) or a **Raspberry Fool** (page 70) at snacktime.

PASSOVER

Passover—one of the most important Jewish holidays—celebrates the people of Israel's freedom from slavery in Egypt. It is a "movable" holiday, occurring in late March or early April.

■ Several books which explain the customs and rituals of Passover are *Passover* by Norma Simon, *Easter and Other Spring Holidays* by Gilda Berger, and *A Picture Book of Jewish Holidays* by David Adler. Celebrate with a **Passover Sponge Cake** (page 70).

EASTER

■ Follow up a reading of *The Adventures of Egbert the Easter Egg* by Richard Armour or *Easter Bunny's Lost Egg* by Sharon Gordon by dyeing Easter eggs. Use the **Easter Egg Dye** recipe (page 71) to turn the coloring of eggs into a real science lesson. After the eggs are dyed, let your students participate in an Easter Egg Roll. Divide the class into two teams and have each team member roll an egg across the room with his or her nose.

■ Bring out the cotton balls for Easter games, arts, and crafts. Cotton balls can be used to represent the Easter Bunny's tail or to play a game of "Pin the Tail on the Bunny." Books to accompany Easter games include *The Easter Bunny That Overslept* by Priscilla and Otto Friedrich and *The Easter Bunny's Secret* by Kathy Darling. Such treats as **Cotton Tail Puffs** (page 72) and **Honey Bunny Biscuits** (page 72) are sure to be hits during this time of year.

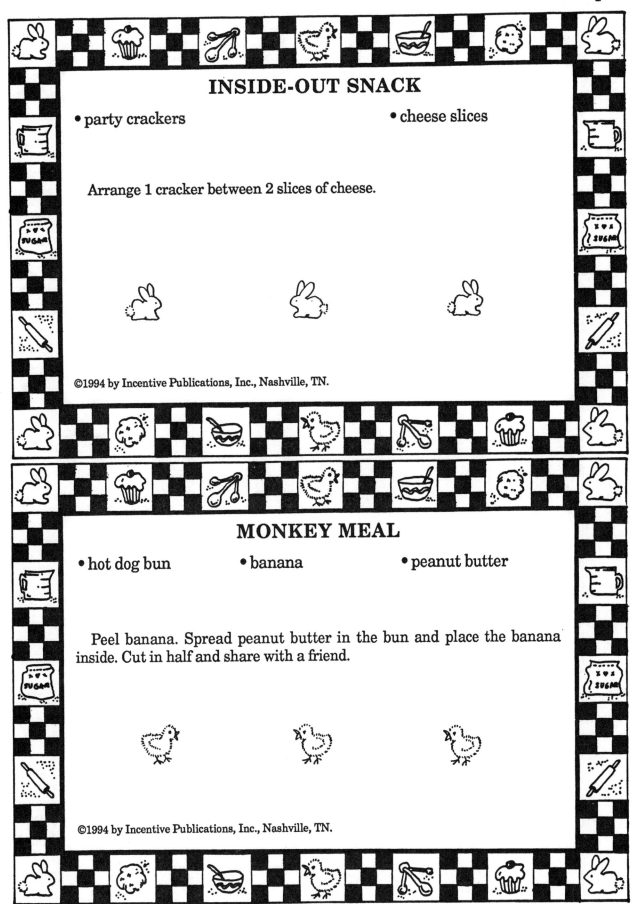

INSIDE-OUT SNACK

- party crackers
- cheese slices

Arrange 1 cracker between 2 slices of cheese.

MONKEY MEAL

- hot dog bun
- banana
- peanut butter

Peel banana. Spread peanut butter in the bun and place the banana inside. Cut in half and share with a friend.

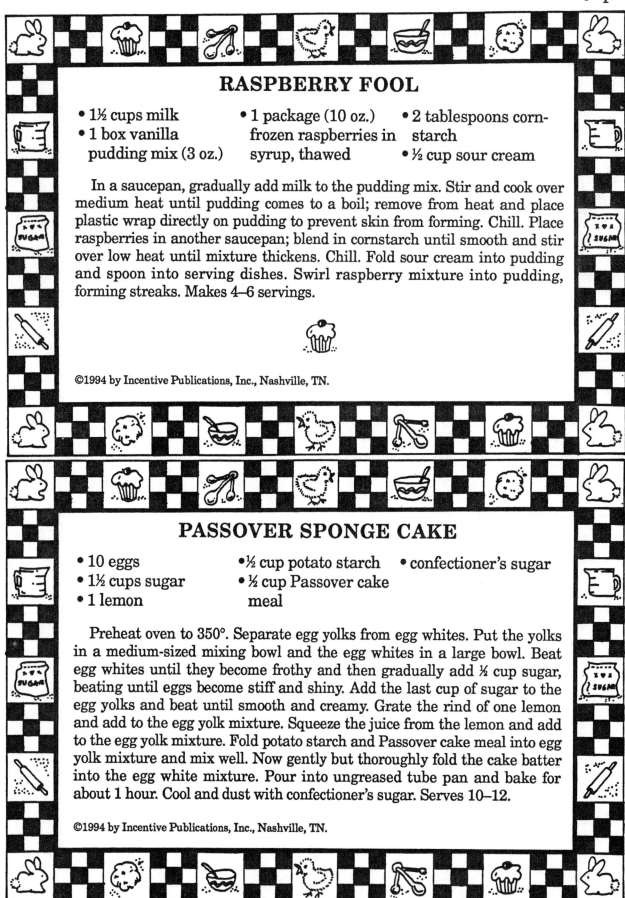

RASPBERRY FOOL

- 1½ cups milk
- 1 box vanilla pudding mix (3 oz.)
- 1 package (10 oz.) frozen raspberries in syrup, thawed
- 2 tablespoons cornstarch
- ½ cup sour cream

In a saucepan, gradually add milk to the pudding mix. Stir and cook over medium heat until pudding comes to a boil; remove from heat and place plastic wrap directly on pudding to prevent skin from forming. Chill. Place raspberries in another saucepan; blend in cornstarch until smooth and stir over low heat until mixture thickens. Chill. Fold sour cream into pudding and spoon into serving dishes. Swirl raspberry mixture into pudding, forming streaks. Makes 4–6 servings.

©1994 by Incentive Publications, Inc., Nashville, TN.

PASSOVER SPONGE CAKE

- 10 eggs
- 1½ cups sugar
- 1 lemon
- ½ cup potato starch
- ½ cup Passover cake meal
- confectioner's sugar

Preheat oven to 350°. Separate egg yolks from egg whites. Put the yolks in a medium-sized mixing bowl and the egg whites in a large bowl. Beat egg whites until they become frothy and then gradually add ½ cup sugar, beating until eggs become stiff and shiny. Add the last cup of sugar to the egg yolks and beat until smooth and creamy. Grate the rind of one lemon and add to the egg yolk mixture. Squeeze the juice from the lemon and add to the egg yolk mixture. Fold potato starch and Passover cake meal into egg yolk mixture and mix well. Now gently but thoroughly fold the cake batter into the egg white mixture. Pour into ungreased tube pan and bake for about 1 hour. Cool and dust with confectioner's sugar. Serves 10–12.

©1994 by Incentive Publications, Inc., Nashville, TN.

UNLEAVENED BREAD (FLAT BREAD)

- 1 cup bread flour
- 1½ cups whole wheat flour
- 1 cup instant oats
- ½ cup oil
- 1 cup boiling water
- ½ teaspoon salt
- 2 tablespoons brown sugar

Combine flour and oats in a large bowl. Boil water and add oil, salt, and brown sugar to the water. Stir in flour and oat mixture. Use enough water to make dough soft, but not too sticky. Knead for 5 minutes. Divide the dough into 12 equal parts and roll each piece paper thin. Cook on top of the stove in an ungreased skillet or griddle, turning once to cook bread on both sides. Cook until crisp and tender.

EASTER EGG DYE

- red beets
- spinach
- cranberries
- blackberries
- yellow onions
- hard-boiled eggs

In separate pots, boil each fruit and vegetable in a small amount of water. This will make a natural dye for eggs. Put each egg in the toe of a clean nylon stocking and dip into the dye. Let sit for several minutes. The longer the egg sits in dye the brighter the color. Remove from stocking and place on paper towel to dry.

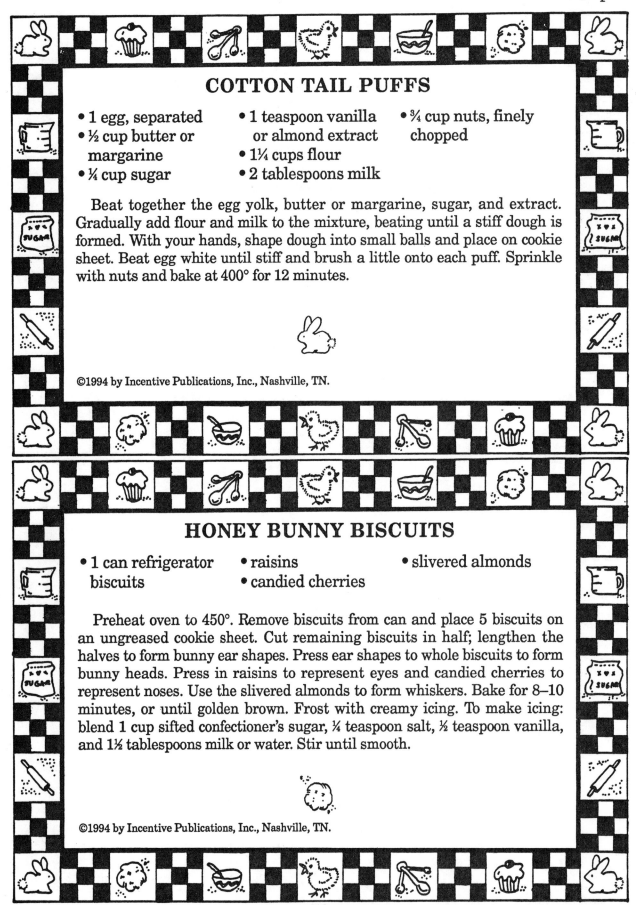

COTTON TAIL PUFFS

- 1 egg, separated
- ½ cup butter or margarine
- ¼ cup sugar
- 1 teaspoon vanilla or almond extract
- 1¼ cups flour
- 2 tablespoons milk
- ¾ cup nuts, finely chopped

Beat together the egg yolk, butter or margarine, sugar, and extract. Gradually add flour and milk to the mixture, beating until a stiff dough is formed. With your hands, shape dough into small balls and place on cookie sheet. Beat egg white until stiff and brush a little onto each puff. Sprinkle with nuts and bake at 400° for 12 minutes.

HONEY BUNNY BISCUITS

- 1 can refrigerator biscuits
- raisins
- candied cherries
- slivered almonds

Preheat oven to 450°. Remove biscuits from can and place 5 biscuits on an ungreased cookie sheet. Cut remaining biscuits in half; lengthen the halves to form bunny ear shapes. Press ear shapes to whole biscuits to form bunny heads. Press in raisins to represent eyes and candied cherries to represent noses. Use the slivered almonds to form whiskers. Bake for 8–10 minutes, or until golden brown. Frost with creamy icing. To make icing: blend 1 cup sifted confectioner's sugar, ¼ teaspoon salt, ½ teaspoon vanilla, and 1½ tablespoons milk or water. Stir until smooth.

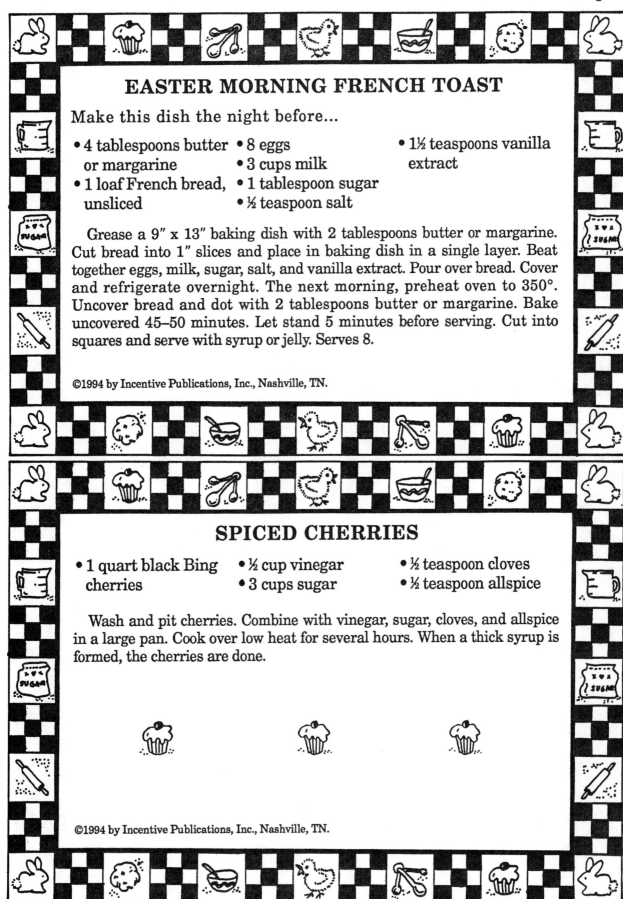

EASTER MORNING FRENCH TOAST

Make this dish the night before...

- 4 tablespoons butter or margarine
- 1 loaf French bread, unsliced
- 8 eggs
- 3 cups milk
- 1 tablespoon sugar
- ½ teaspoon salt
- 1½ teaspoons vanilla extract

Grease a 9" x 13" baking dish with 2 tablespoons butter or margarine. Cut bread into 1" slices and place in baking dish in a single layer. Beat together eggs, milk, sugar, salt, and vanilla extract. Pour over bread. Cover and refrigerate overnight. The next morning, preheat oven to 350°. Uncover bread and dot with 2 tablespoons butter or margarine. Bake uncovered 45–50 minutes. Let stand 5 minutes before serving. Cut into squares and serve with syrup or jelly. Serves 8.

SPICED CHERRIES

- 1 quart black Bing cherries
- ½ cup vinegar
- 3 cups sugar
- ½ teaspoon cloves
- ½ teaspoon allspice

Wash and pit cherries. Combine with vinegar, sugar, cloves, and allspice in a large pan. Cook over low heat for several hours. When a thick syrup is formed, the cherries are done.

Summer Months

MOTHER'S DAY

■ **Mother's Special Tea** (page 76) and **Chocolate-Covered Pretzels** (page 77) always make welcome Mother's Day gifts. Two books that cover the subject of Mother's Day are *Mother's Day* by Mary Kay Phelan and *The Mommy Exchange* by Amy Hest. A challenging activity would be for each child to write a poem to his or her mother after listening to some examples in Myra Livingstone's book *Poems for Mothers*.

INDEPENDENCE DAY

■ Holding a parade and making paper flags, noise makers, hats, and streamers are super warm-weather activities. After an Independence Day parade, make a patriotic **Red, White, and Blue Salad** (page 77) and a pitcher of icy cold **Real Lemonade** (page 78).

■ Two wonderful books with information about the American flag are *The Great Book of Flags* by David White and *Let's Find Out About Our Flag* by Charles Shapp. *I Pledge Allegiance* by June Swanson and *The Story of the Statue of Liberty* by Natalie Miller are also books with patriotic themes.

SUMMER

■ Summer school can be made fun with a plate of **Ants on a Log** (page 79) and the stories *A Picnic, Hurrah!* by Franz Brandenberg and *Summer Days* by Roger Pare. Continue the ant theme by singing this song to the tune of "When Johnny Comes Marching Home":

> *The ants go walking round and round,*
> *Hurrah, hurrah.*
> *The ants go walking round and round,*
> *Hurrah, hurrah.*
> *The ants go walking round and round;*
> *They creep and crawl upon the ground.*
> *And they all move closer,*
> *Eyeing your picnic feast.*

Let children make up additional lyrics to this and other tunes—they will have loads of fun! After singing, you might have the children try to locate a missing picnic basket that you have hidden. Feed them **Banana Sandwiches** (page 82) and **Hide-and-Seek Pudding** (page 83) to continue the summer excitement.

OTHER BOOKS FOR SUMMER MONTHS

Bugs by Nancy Winslow Parker and Joan Richards Wright.

Fannie's Fruit by Leslie Kimmelman.

Fireflies by Julie Brinckloe.

Henry's Fourth of July by Holly Keller.

The Teddy Bear's Picnic by Jimmy Kennedy.

The Very Hungry Caterpillar by Eric Carle.

The Very Quiet Cricket by Eric Carle.

MOTHER'S SPECIAL TEA

- 12 oz. orange drink mix
- 2 cups sugar
- 1 cup instant tea mix, dry
- 1 package lemonade mix, dry
- 2 teaspoons cinnamon
- ½ teaspoon cloves

Mix all ingredients together and store in a glass jar. To serve, mix 1 tablespoon of mixture per cup of hot water.

HUGS AND KISSES

- square crackers
- spreadable cheese or peanut butter
- small pieces of the following vegetables: carrot, green pepper, celery, cucumber, and radish

Spread cheese or peanut butter on the crackers. Design x's and o's on the tops of the crackers using the vegetable slices.

CHOCOLATE-COVERED PRETZELS

- 1 cup semi-sweet chocolate chips
- 1 bar (4 oz.) milk chocolate, broken
- 2 tablespoons shortening
- 1 package (9–10 oz.) unsalted pretzels

Combine chocolate chips, chocolate bar pieces, and shortening in a saucepan. Melt over low heat. Use a fork to dip pretzels in melted chocolate. Place coated pretzels on cookie sheet covered with wax paper. Chill for 15–30 minutes or until chocolate is firm.

RED, WHITE, AND BLUE SALAD

- strawberries
- blueberries
- bananas

Wash and clean fruit. Arrange in a bowl and mix gently. It might be fun to eat this snack outdoors.

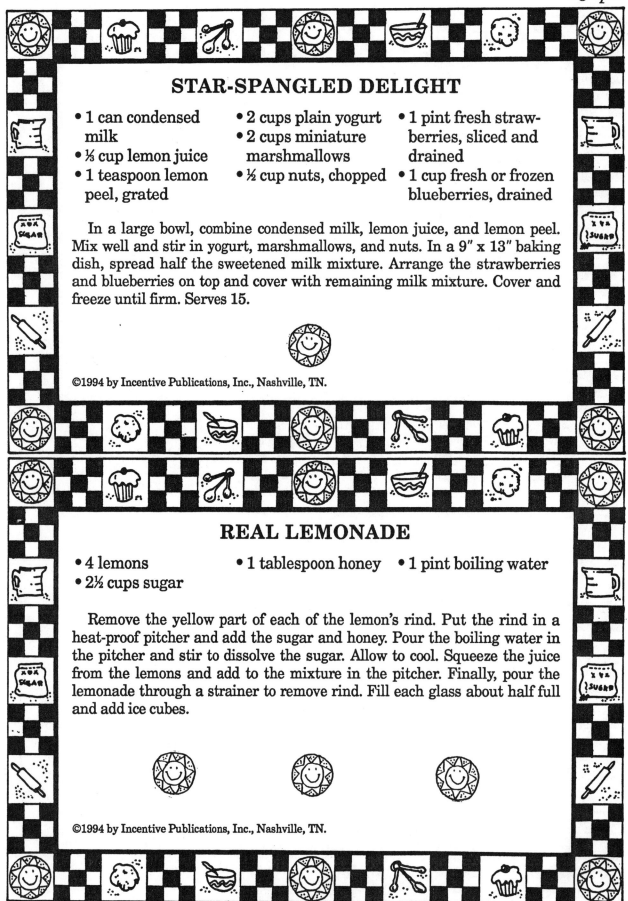

STAR-SPANGLED DELIGHT

- 1 can condensed milk
- ⅓ cup lemon juice
- 1 teaspoon lemon peel, grated

- 2 cups plain yogurt
- 2 cups miniature marshmallows
- ½ cup nuts, chopped

- 1 pint fresh strawberries, sliced and drained
- 1 cup fresh or frozen blueberries, drained

In a large bowl, combine condensed milk, lemon juice, and lemon peel. Mix well and stir in yogurt, marshmallows, and nuts. In a 9" x 13" baking dish, spread half the sweetened milk mixture. Arrange the strawberries and blueberries on top and cover with remaining milk mixture. Cover and freeze until firm. Serves 15.

REAL LEMONADE

- 4 lemons
- 2½ cups sugar

- 1 tablespoon honey

- 1 pint boiling water

Remove the yellow part of each of the lemon's rind. Put the rind in a heat-proof pitcher and add the sugar and honey. Pour the boiling water in the pitcher and stir to dissolve the sugar. Allow to cool. Squeeze the juice from the lemons and add to the mixture in the pitcher. Finally, pour the lemonade through a strainer to remove rind. Fill each glass about half full and add ice cubes.

FRUIT KABOBS

- cantaloupe cubes
- honeydew cubes
- grapes
- strawberries
- cheddar cheese cubes
- farmer cheese cubes

Place mixture of fruits and cheeses on wooden skewers in colorful combinations. Chill until serving time.

ANTS ON A LOG

- 1 apple
- peanut butter
- raisins

Cut apple into quarters. Remove core and seeds. Top each quarter with peanut butter and raisins. Serves one.

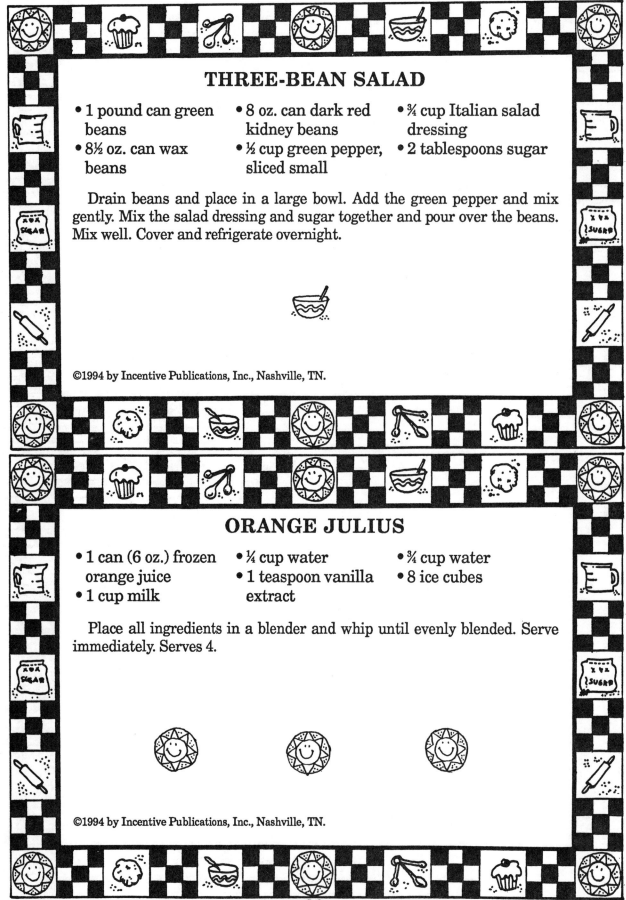

THREE-BEAN SALAD

- 1 pound can green beans
- 8½ oz. can wax beans
- 8 oz. can dark red kidney beans
- ½ cup green pepper, sliced small
- ¾ cup Italian salad dressing
- 2 tablespoons sugar

Drain beans and place in a large bowl. Add the green pepper and mix gently. Mix the salad dressing and sugar together and pour over the beans. Mix well. Cover and refrigerate overnight.

ORANGE JULIUS

- 1 can (6 oz.) frozen orange juice
- 1 cup milk
- ¼ cup water
- 1 teaspoon vanilla extract
- ¾ cup water
- 8 ice cubes

Place all ingredients in a blender and whip until evenly blended. Serve immediately. Serves 4.

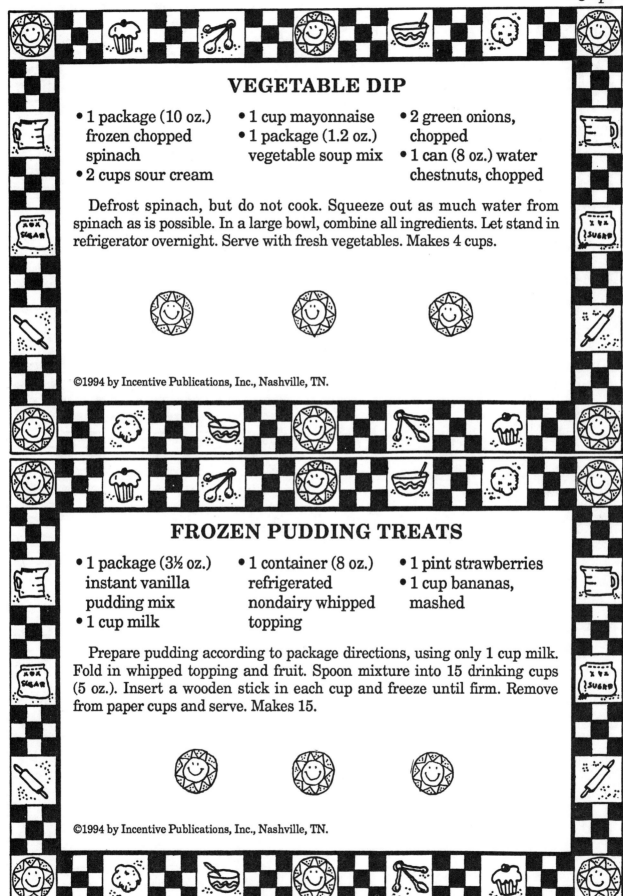

VEGETABLE DIP

- 1 package (10 oz.) frozen chopped spinach
- 2 cups sour cream
- 1 cup mayonnaise
- 1 package (1.2 oz.) vegetable soup mix
- 2 green onions, chopped
- 1 can (8 oz.) water chestnuts, chopped

Defrost spinach, but do not cook. Squeeze out as much water from spinach as is possible. In a large bowl, combine all ingredients. Let stand in refrigerator overnight. Serve with fresh vegetables. Makes 4 cups.

FROZEN PUDDING TREATS

- 1 package (3½ oz.) instant vanilla pudding mix
- 1 cup milk
- 1 container (8 oz.) refrigerated nondairy whipped topping
- 1 pint strawberries
- 1 cup bananas, mashed

Prepare pudding according to package directions, using only 1 cup milk. Fold in whipped topping and fruit. Spoon mixture into 15 drinking cups (5 oz.). Insert a wooden stick in each cup and freeze until firm. Remove from paper cups and serve. Makes 15.

JULY FOURTH PUDDING

- 1 package whipped cream dessert topping mix
- ½ cup milk
- ¼ cup sugar
- ½ teaspoon vanilla extract
- red and blue decorating sugar
- ⅓ cup shredded coconut

Combine the whipped topping mix with milk and beat until stiff. Add the sugar and vanilla extract. Beat until sugar is blended. Place 6 paper muffin cups in a muffin tin and spoon the pudding into them. Freeze until firm. When ready to serve, remove the paper cups and place the pudding on plates. Sprinkle each with red sugar on one side, blue on the other, and coconut in the middle.

BANANA SANDWICH

- 2 cups peanut butter
- 4 bananas
- 52 graham crackers

Combine peanut butter and bananas in bowl, mixing well. Chill. Spread 2 tablespoons of the mixture onto each graham cracker square. Cover each square with a second square. Wrap each individually in foil. Freeze for several hours. (Yield: 26 sandwiches.)

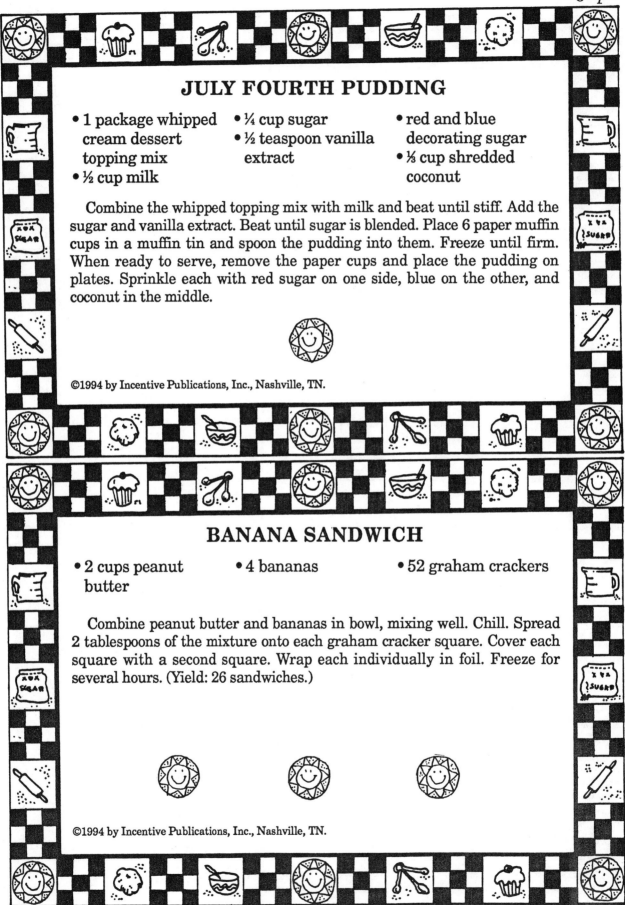

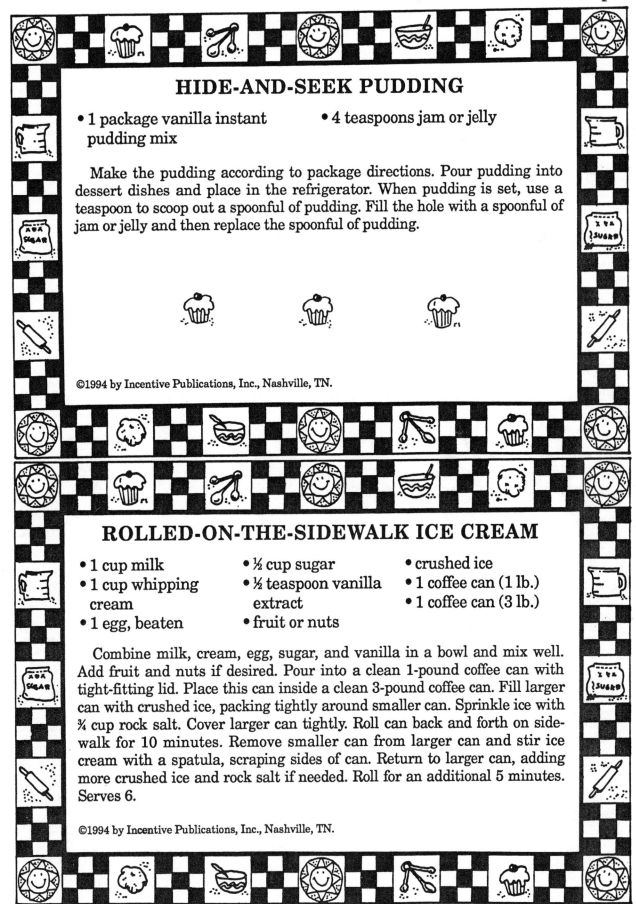

HIDE-AND-SEEK PUDDING

- 1 package vanilla instant pudding mix
- 4 teaspoons jam or jelly

Make the pudding according to package directions. Pour pudding into dessert dishes and place in the refrigerator. When pudding is set, use a teaspoon to scoop out a spoonful of pudding. Fill the hole with a spoonful of jam or jelly and then replace the spoonful of pudding.

ROLLED-ON-THE-SIDEWALK ICE CREAM

- 1 cup milk
- 1 cup whipping cream
- 1 egg, beaten
- ½ cup sugar
- ½ teaspoon vanilla extract
- fruit or nuts
- crushed ice
- 1 coffee can (1 lb.)
- 1 coffee can (3 lb.)

Combine milk, cream, egg, sugar, and vanilla in a bowl and mix well. Add fruit and nuts if desired. Pour into a clean 1-pound coffee can with tight-fitting lid. Place this can inside a clean 3-pound coffee can. Fill larger can with crushed ice, packing tightly around smaller can. Sprinkle ice with ¾ cup rock salt. Cover larger can tightly. Roll can back and forth on sidewalk for 10 minutes. Remove smaller can from larger can and stir ice cream with a spatula, scraping sides of can. Return to larger can, adding more crushed ice and rock salt if needed. Roll for an additional 5 minutes. Serves 6.

Colors

■ Combine reading and cooking with a lesson in learning color names. For very young learners, you might choose to institute a Color Week, during which time the children wear designated colors to class, make food of a specific color for snacktime, bring items of a particular color for show-and-tell, etc. Kids will love eating brightly-colored **Orange Snow** (page 88), luscious yellow **Lemonade Pie** (page 89), and **Very Blue Berry Pie** (page 92).

■ For older students, the process of mixing two colors together to make a new color takes on added meaning when students can eat the results of their experiment. One way to accomplish this is by making **Easy Icing**: cream together 1 cup butter-flavored vegetable shortening, 1 can condensed milk, and 1 egg white. Beat with an electric

mixer for 10 minutes until icing is fluffy. Separate into two bowls. Tint one half with yellow food coloring and the other half with blue food coloring. Hand each student a graham cracker to which has been added a small amount of yellow icing and a small amount of blue icing on its corners. Allow each student to spread together the blue and yellow icing to make green icing.

BOOKS FOR COLORS

Color Zoo by Lois Ehlert.

Harold and the Purple Crayon by Crockett Johnson.

If You Had a Paintbrush by Fulvio Testa.

Mary Wore Her Red Dress, and Henry Wore His Green Sneakers by Merle Peek.

Mouse Paint by Ellen Stall Walsh.

My Red Umbrella by Robert Bright.

Pinkish, Purplish, Bluish Egg by Bill Peet.

The Red Ripe Strawberry and the Big Hungry Bear by Audrey and Don Wood.

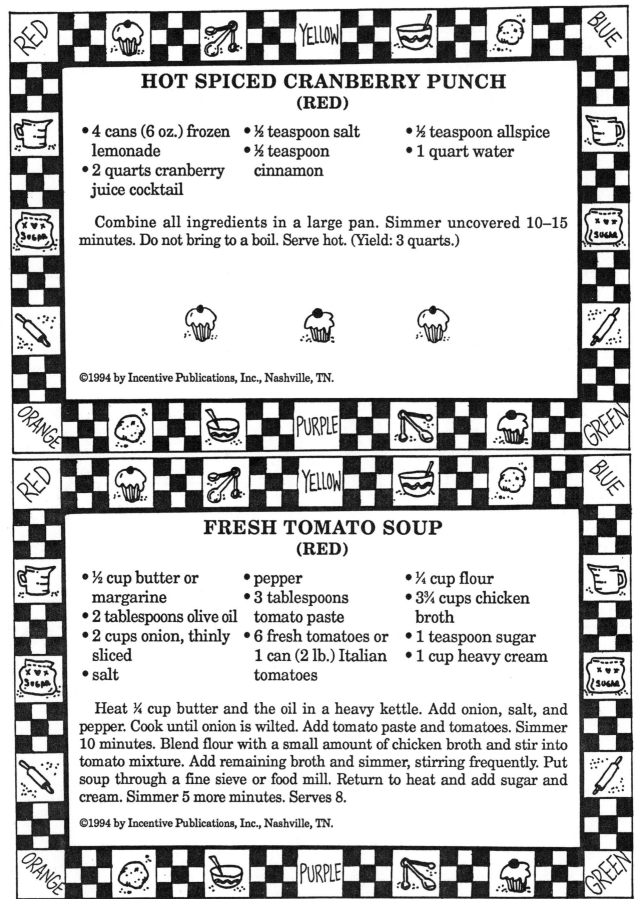

HOT SPICED CRANBERRY PUNCH
(RED)

- 4 cans (6 oz.) frozen lemonade
- 2 quarts cranberry juice cocktail
- ½ teaspoon salt
- ½ teaspoon cinnamon
- ½ teaspoon allspice
- 1 quart water

Combine all ingredients in a large pan. Simmer uncovered 10–15 minutes. Do not bring to a boil. Serve hot. (Yield: 3 quarts.)

FRESH TOMATO SOUP
(RED)

- ½ cup butter or margarine
- 2 tablespoons olive oil
- 2 cups onion, thinly sliced
- salt
- pepper
- 3 tablespoons tomato paste
- 6 fresh tomatoes or 1 can (2 lb.) Italian tomatoes
- ¼ cup flour
- 3¾ cups chicken broth
- 1 teaspoon sugar
- 1 cup heavy cream

Heat ¼ cup butter and the oil in a heavy kettle. Add onion, salt, and pepper. Cook until onion is wilted. Add tomato paste and tomatoes. Simmer 10 minutes. Blend flour with a small amount of chicken broth and stir into tomato mixture. Add remaining broth and simmer, stirring frequently. Put soup through a fine sieve or food mill. Return to heat and add sugar and cream. Simmer 5 more minutes. Serves 8.

GRANDMA'S CINNAMON APPLES
(RED)

- 10 Jonathan or Rome Beauty apples
- 1 cup red cinnamon candies
- 1 cup water
- 2 drops red food coloring
- marshmallows

Core and peel apples, leaving a ½" strip of peel around the middle to hold apples together. Place the cinnamon candies, water, and red food coloring in a large skillet and bring to a boil. Cook until mixture is somewhat thick. Place apples in boiling syrup and cook, continually spooning syrup over apples. Apples should pierce easily with a fork when done, about 10 minutes. Remove from heat and fill center of each apple with pieces of marshmallow. Pour remaining syrup over tops of apples and serve. Leftover syrup is great over ice cream, too.

COPPER PENNY SALAD
(ORANGE)

- 2 pounds carrots
- ½ cup sugar
- 1 can tomato soup
- ½ cup vinegar
- ½ cup cooking oil
- 1 small onion, chopped
- ½ cup green pepper, chopped
- salt and pepper

Slice carrots and cook until just tender. Mix remaining ingredients together and pour over carrots. Let stand in refrigerator for several hours or overnight.

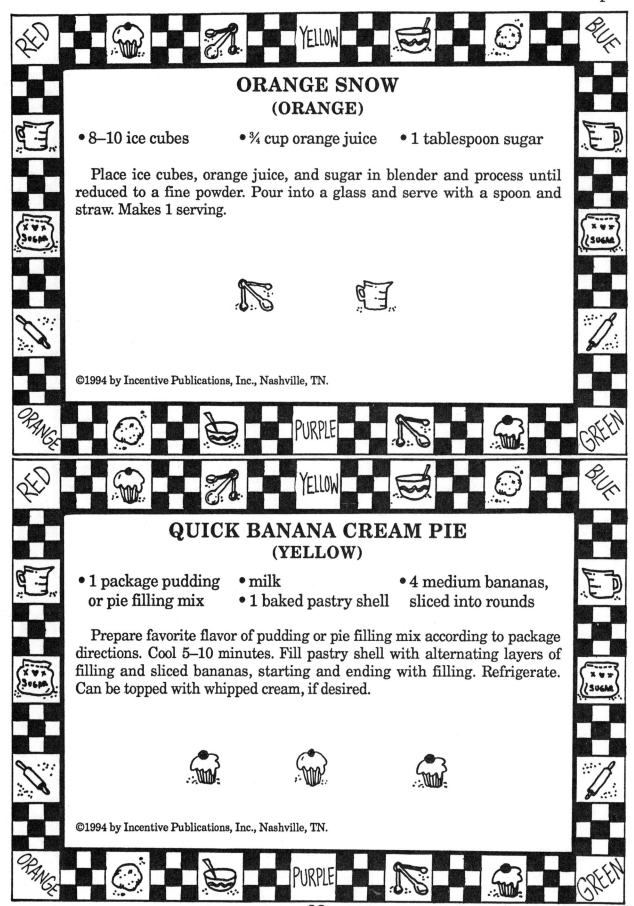

ORANGE SNOW
(ORANGE)

- 8–10 ice cubes
- ¾ cup orange juice
- 1 tablespoon sugar

Place ice cubes, orange juice, and sugar in blender and process until reduced to a fine powder. Pour into a glass and serve with a spoon and straw. Makes 1 serving.

QUICK BANANA CREAM PIE
(YELLOW)

- 1 package pudding or pie filling mix
- milk
- 1 baked pastry shell
- 4 medium bananas, sliced into rounds

Prepare favorite flavor of pudding or pie filling mix according to package directions. Cool 5–10 minutes. Fill pastry shell with alternating layers of filling and sliced bananas, starting and ending with filling. Refrigerate. Can be topped with whipped cream, if desired.

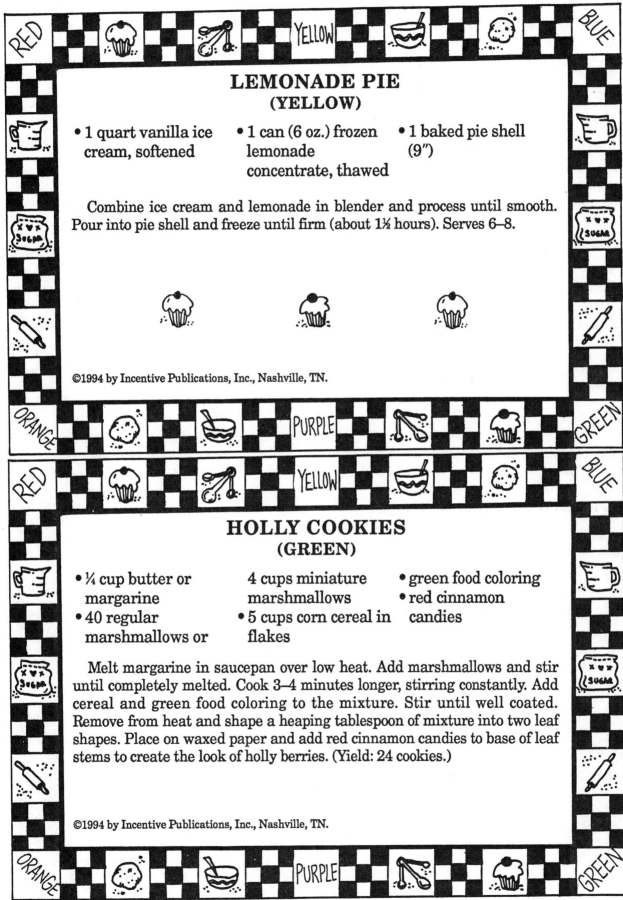

LEMONADE PIE
(YELLOW)

- 1 quart vanilla ice cream, softened
- 1 can (6 oz.) frozen lemonade concentrate, thawed
- 1 baked pie shell (9″)

Combine ice cream and lemonade in blender and process until smooth. Pour into pie shell and freeze until firm (about 1½ hours). Serves 6–8.

HOLLY COOKIES
(GREEN)

- ¼ cup butter or margarine
- 40 regular marshmallows or
- 4 cups miniature marshmallows
- 5 cups corn cereal in flakes
- green food coloring
- red cinnamon candies

Melt margarine in saucepan over low heat. Add marshmallows and stir until completely melted. Cook 3–4 minutes longer, stirring constantly. Add cereal and green food coloring to the mixture. Stir until well coated. Remove from heat and shape a heaping tablespoon of mixture into two leaf shapes. Place on waxed paper and add red cinnamon candies to base of leaf stems to create the look of holly berries. (Yield: 24 cookies.)

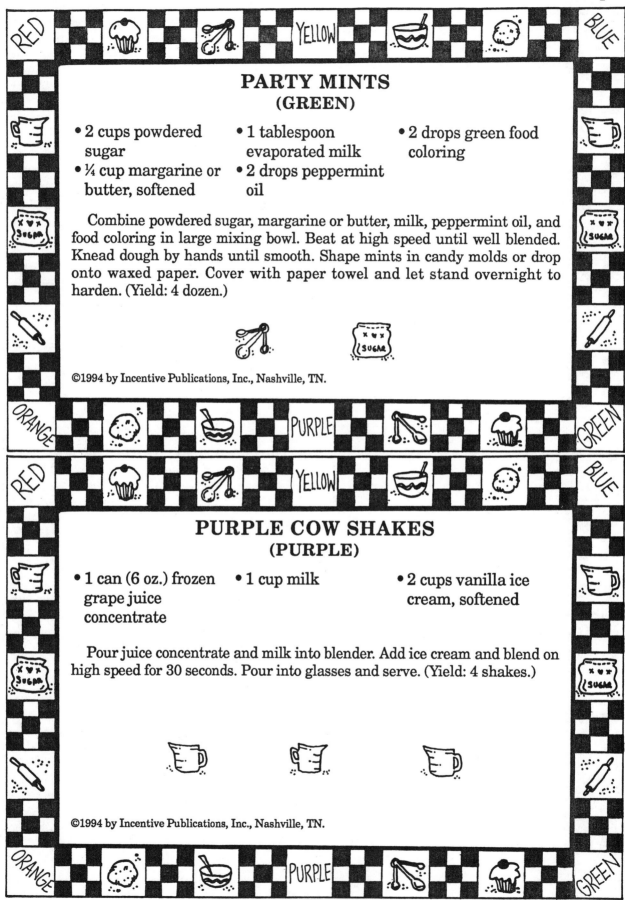

PARTY MINTS
(GREEN)

- 2 cups powdered sugar
- ¼ cup margarine or butter, softened
- 1 tablespoon evaporated milk
- 2 drops peppermint oil
- 2 drops green food coloring

Combine powdered sugar, margarine or butter, milk, peppermint oil, and food coloring in large mixing bowl. Beat at high speed until well blended. Knead dough by hands until smooth. Shape mints in candy molds or drop onto waxed paper. Cover with paper towel and let stand overnight to harden. (Yield: 4 dozen.)

PURPLE COW SHAKES
(PURPLE)

- 1 can (6 oz.) frozen grape juice concentrate
- 1 cup milk
- 2 cups vanilla ice cream, softened

Pour juice concentrate and milk into blender. Add ice cream and blend on high speed for 30 seconds. Pour into glasses and serve. (Yield: 4 shakes.)

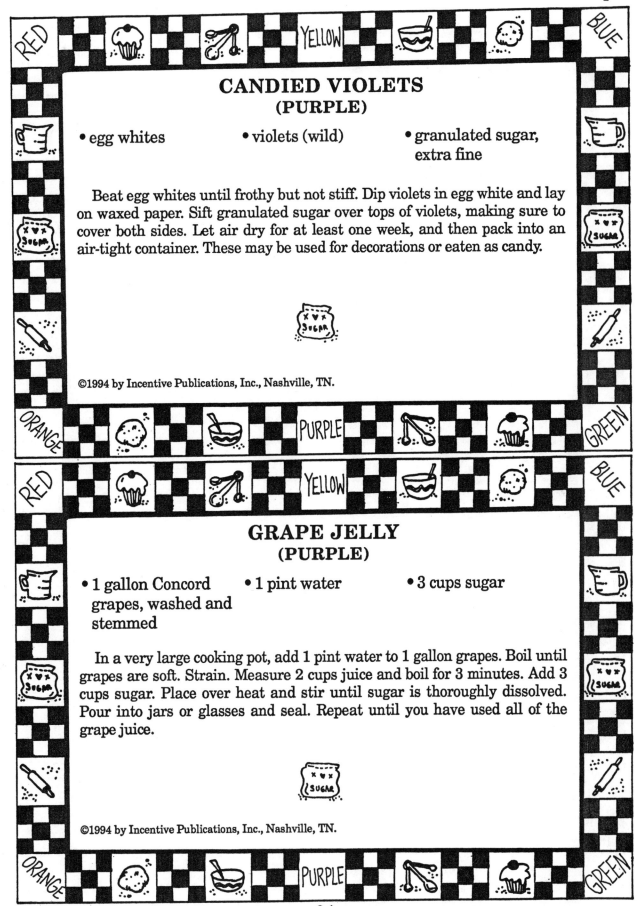

CANDIED VIOLETS
(PURPLE)

- egg whites
- violets (wild)
- granulated sugar, extra fine

Beat egg whites until frothy but not stiff. Dip violets in egg white and lay on waxed paper. Sift granulated sugar over tops of violets, making sure to cover both sides. Let air dry for at least one week, and then pack into an air-tight container. These may be used for decorations or eaten as candy.

GRAPE JELLY
(PURPLE)

- 1 gallon Concord grapes, washed and stemmed
- 1 pint water
- 3 cups sugar

In a very large cooking pot, add 1 pint water to 1 gallon grapes. Boil until grapes are soft. Strain. Measure 2 cups juice and boil for 3 minutes. Add 3 cups sugar. Place over heat and stir until sugar is thoroughly dissolved. Pour into jars or glasses and seal. Repeat until you have used all of the grape juice.

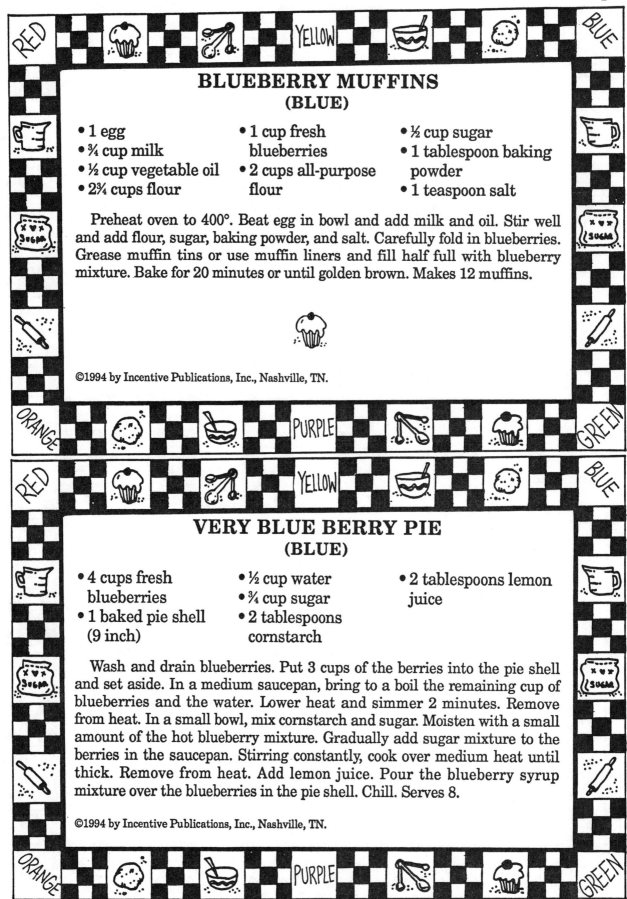

BLUEBERRY MUFFINS
(BLUE)

- 1 egg
- ¾ cup milk
- ½ cup vegetable oil
- 2¾ cups flour
- 1 cup fresh blueberries
- 2 cups all-purpose flour
- ½ cup sugar
- 1 tablespoon baking powder
- 1 teaspoon salt

Preheat oven to 400°. Beat egg in bowl and add milk and oil. Stir well and add flour, sugar, baking powder, and salt. Carefully fold in blueberries. Grease muffin tins or use muffin liners and fill half full with blueberry mixture. Bake for 20 minutes or until golden brown. Makes 12 muffins.

VERY BLUE BERRY PIE
(BLUE)

- 4 cups fresh blueberries
- 1 baked pie shell (9 inch)
- ½ cup water
- ¾ cup sugar
- 2 tablespoons cornstarch
- 2 tablespoons lemon juice

Wash and drain blueberries. Put 3 cups of the berries into the pie shell and set aside. In a medium saucepan, bring to a boil the remaining cup of blueberries and the water. Lower heat and simmer 2 minutes. Remove from heat. In a small bowl, mix cornstarch and sugar. Moisten with a small amount of the hot blueberry mixture. Gradually add sugar mixture to the berries in the saucepan. Stirring constantly, cook over medium heat until thick. Remove from heat. Add lemon juice. Pour the blueberry syrup mixture over the blueberries in the pie shell. Chill. Serves 8.

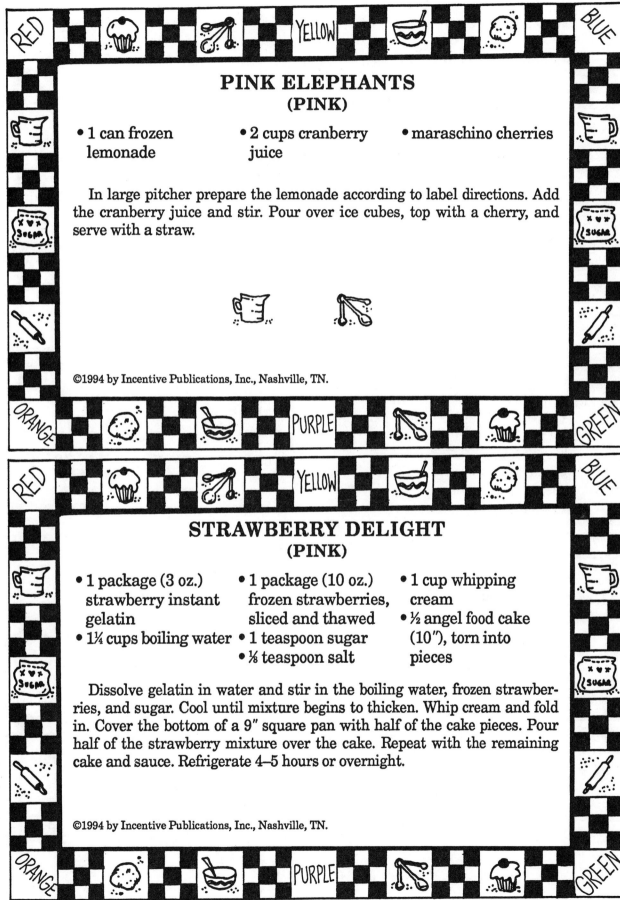

PINK ELEPHANTS
(PINK)

- 1 can frozen lemonade
- 2 cups cranberry juice
- maraschino cherries

In large pitcher prepare the lemonade according to label directions. Add the cranberry juice and stir. Pour over ice cubes, top with a cherry, and serve with a straw.

STRAWBERRY DELIGHT
(PINK)

- 1 package (3 oz.) strawberry instant gelatin
- 1¼ cups boiling water
- 1 package (10 oz.) frozen strawberries, sliced and thawed
- 1 teaspoon sugar
- ⅛ teaspoon salt
- 1 cup whipping cream
- ½ angel food cake (10″), torn into pieces

Dissolve gelatin in water and stir in the boiling water, frozen strawberries, and sugar. Cool until mixture begins to thicken. Whip cream and fold in. Cover the bottom of a 9″ square pan with half of the cake pieces. Pour half of the strawberry mixture over the cake. Repeat with the remaining cake and sauce. Refrigerate 4–5 hours or overnight.

TOUCH DOWNS
(BROWN)

- 1 package (6 oz.) chocolate chips
- 2 tablespoons shortening
- ¼ teaspoon cinnamon
- ⅛ teaspoon nutmeg
- shredded wheat cereal, small pieces

Melt chocolate chips and shortening together. Add cinnamon and nutmeg and mix well. Coat each piece of shredded wheat with chocolate. Place on waxed paper and let stand until chocolate has hardened. Makes about 6 dozen.

MUD PIE
(BROWN)

- 1 package (1 lb.) cream-filled chocolate sandwich cookies
- 1 stick butter or margarine, melted
- 2 tablespoons butter or margarine
- 2 oz. unsweetened chocolate
- 1 cup sugar
- 1 can (5½ oz.) evaporated milk
- 2 pints ice cream, softened
- semi-sweet chocolate, shaved

Scrape filling from sandwich cookies. Crush cookies and mix with butter. Press into 9″ pie plate. Chill. Melt together 2 tablespoons butter and chocolate. Stir in sugar and milk. Cook, stirring over medium heat until thick. Cool. Spoon 1 pint ice cream into pie shell. Top with half of the fudge sauce. Freeze. Repeat with ice cream and sauce and refreeze. Thaw 15 minutes before serving. Serves 8–10.

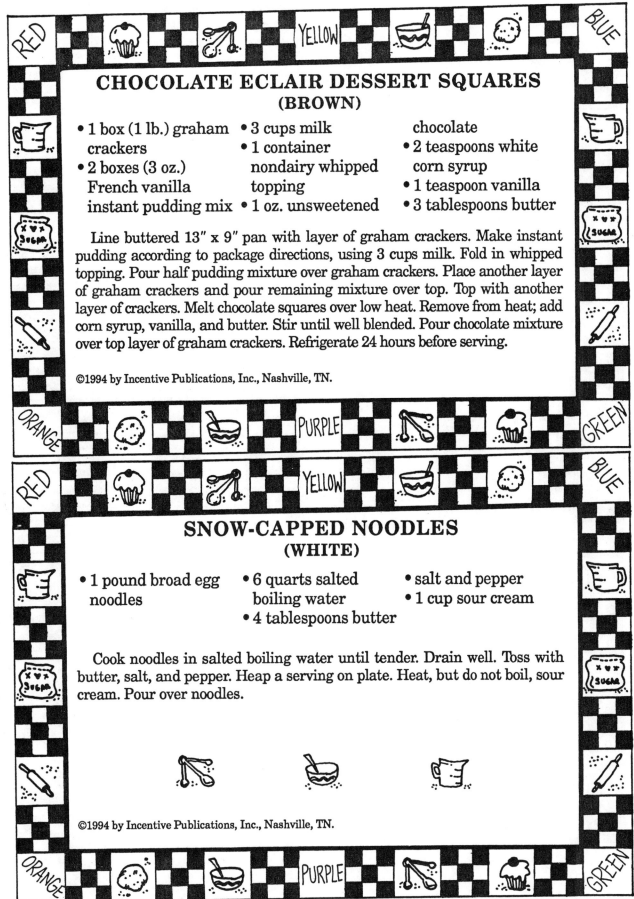

CHOCOLATE ECLAIR DESSERT SQUARES
(BROWN)

- 1 box (1 lb.) graham crackers
- 2 boxes (3 oz.) French vanilla instant pudding mix
- 3 cups milk
- 1 container nondairy whipped topping
- 1 oz. unsweetened chocolate
- 2 teaspoons white corn syrup
- 1 teaspoon vanilla
- 3 tablespoons butter

Line buttered 13" x 9" pan with layer of graham crackers. Make instant pudding according to package directions, using 3 cups milk. Fold in whipped topping. Pour half pudding mixture over graham crackers. Place another layer of graham crackers and pour remaining mixture over top. Top with another layer of crackers. Melt chocolate squares over low heat. Remove from heat; add corn syrup, vanilla, and butter. Stir until well blended. Pour chocolate mixture over top layer of graham crackers. Refrigerate 24 hours before serving.

©1994 by Incentive Publications, Inc., Nashville, TN.

SNOW-CAPPED NOODLES
(WHITE)

- 1 pound broad egg noodles
- 6 quarts salted boiling water
- 4 tablespoons butter
- salt and pepper
- 1 cup sour cream

Cook noodles in salted boiling water until tender. Drain well. Toss with butter, salt, and pepper. Heap a serving on plate. Heat, but do not boil, sour cream. Pour over noodles.

©1994 by Incentive Publications, Inc., Nashville, TN.

RED · YELLOW · BLUE

CLOUD BISCUITS
(WHITE)

- 2 cups flour
- 1 tablespoon sugar
- 4 teaspoons baking powder
- ½ teaspoon salt
- ½ cup shortening
- 1 egg, slightly beaten
- ⅔ cup buttermilk
- 16 sugar cubes
- ¼ cup orange juice

Preheat oven to 400°. Mix together first 4 ingredients. Cut in shortening with pastry blender. Stir in egg and milk. Knead lightly on a floured surface and roll until ¾" thick. Cut into any shape and place on ungreased cookie sheet. Dip sugar cubes in orange juice and press lightly on top of each biscuit. Bake 12–14 minutes. Serve warm. (Yield: 16 biscuits.)

ORANGE · PURPLE · GREEN

RED · YELLOW · BLUE

COTTAGE CHEESE PANCAKES
(WHITE)

- 1 cup sifted flour
- 1 tablespoon sugar
- ½ teaspoon salt
- sour cream
- cottage cheese
- 2 cups milk
- 3 eggs

Sift together flour, sugar, and salt. Add sour cream, cottage cheese, milk, and eggs. Fold until flour is just moistened. Bake on lightly greased griddle or electric skillet. (Yield: 16 pancakes.)

ORANGE · PURPLE · GREEN

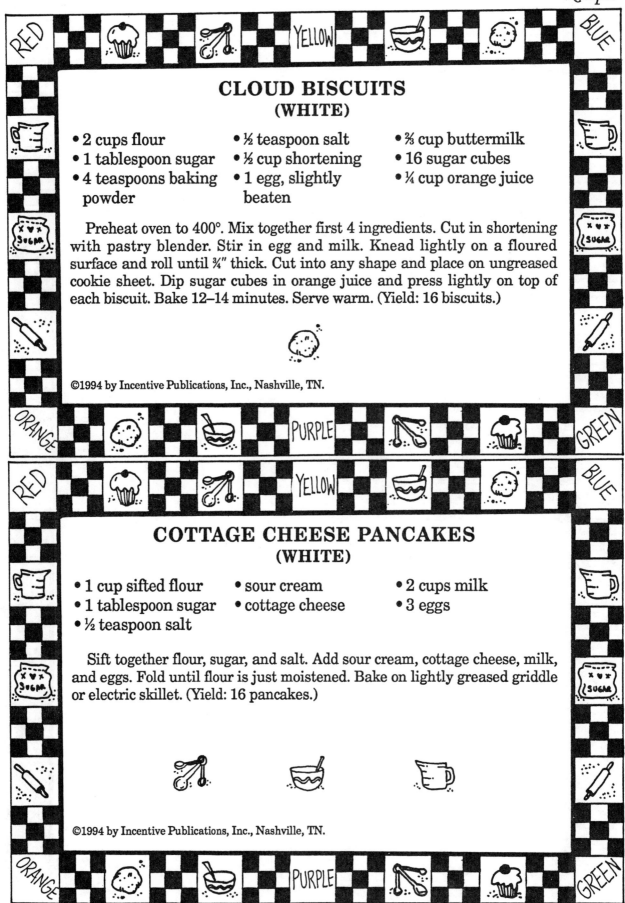

ABC's

By introducing each letter of the alphabet individually while incorporating the following Alphabet Recipes into your lesson plan, you can make learning—and reinforcing—the ABC's fun for all children. The learning experience can be enhanced by introducing each alphabet recipe with a story, art project, music lesson, or physical activity, as in the following example.

■ Make **Doughnuts** (page 100) after children have played dominos, drawn dinosaurs, banged on drums, danced, walked like ducks, growled like dogs, and played a game of dodge ball.

■ For a treat that combines all of the letters of the alphabet, whip up some alphabet soup. Ask each child to identify the letters in his or her bowl of soup. You may want to play a version of the game of Bingo. Call out letters and ask children to identify whether or not they have those particular letters in their servings. This game can also be played with alphabet cereal.

BOOKS FOR ABC'S

Busy, Buzzing Bumblebees and Other Tongue Twisters by Alvin Schwartz

Find Your ABC by Richard Scarry.

APPLE CRUNCH

- 7–9 tart apples
- 1 cup white sugar
- 1 cup brown sugar
- 1 cup flour
- ½ cup butter
- ¼ teaspoon salt
- ¼ teaspoon vanilla extract

Slice apples and place in casserole dish. Stir both types of sugar into sliced apples. Combine remaining ingredients and pour over apples. DO NOT STIR. Bake at 350° for 1 hour. Serves 6.

BLUEBERRY BUCKLE

- ¾ cup sugar
- 4 tablespoons butter
- 1 egg
- 2 teaspoons baking powder
- 2 cups flour
- ½ teaspoon salt
- ½ cup milk
- ½ cup sugar
- 2 cups blueberries
- ⅛ cup flour
- ½ teaspoon cinnamon
- ¼ cup butter, softened

Mix together sugar, butter, and egg and then stir in baking powder, flour, and salt. Mix in milk and sugar alternately and fold in blueberries. Pour into greased and floured 9″ square pan. Cut together the remaining ingredients and sprinkle over batter. Bake at 375° for 30 minutes. Serves 6–8.

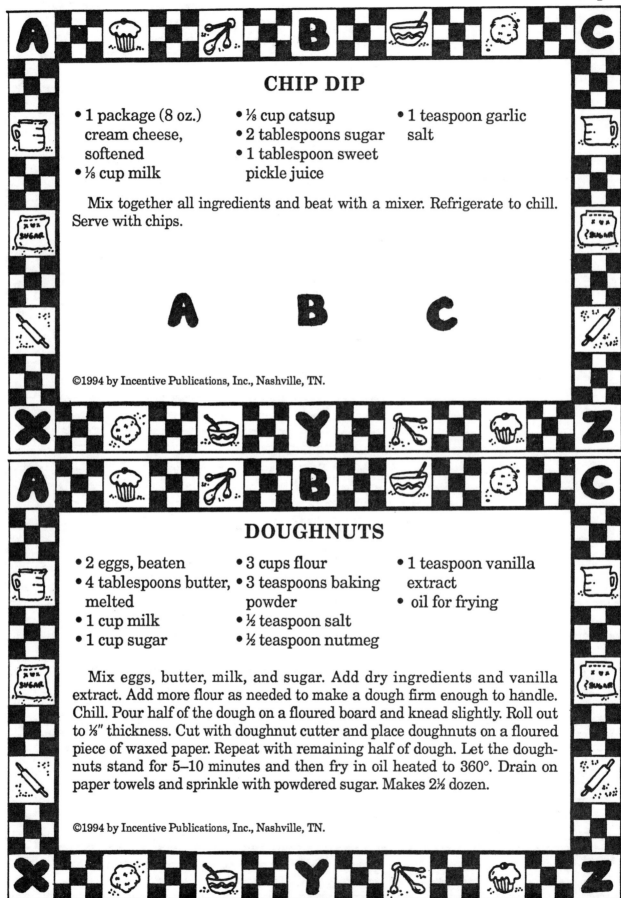

CHIP DIP

- 1 package (8 oz.) cream cheese, softened
- ⅛ cup milk
- ⅛ cup catsup
- 2 tablespoons sugar
- 1 tablespoon sweet pickle juice
- 1 teaspoon garlic salt

Mix together all ingredients and beat with a mixer. Refrigerate to chill. Serve with chips.

DOUGHNUTS

- 2 eggs, beaten
- 4 tablespoons butter, melted
- 1 cup milk
- 1 cup sugar
- 3 cups flour
- 3 teaspoons baking powder
- ½ teaspoon salt
- ½ teaspoon nutmeg
- 1 teaspoon vanilla extract
- oil for frying

Mix eggs, butter, milk, and sugar. Add dry ingredients and vanilla extract. Add more flour as needed to make a dough firm enough to handle. Chill. Pour half of the dough on a floured board and knead slightly. Roll out to ⅛″ thickness. Cut with doughnut cutter and place doughnuts on a floured piece of waxed paper. Repeat with remaining half of dough. Let the doughnuts stand for 5–10 minutes and then fry in oil heated to 360°. Drain on paper towels and sprinkle with powdered sugar. Makes 2½ dozen.

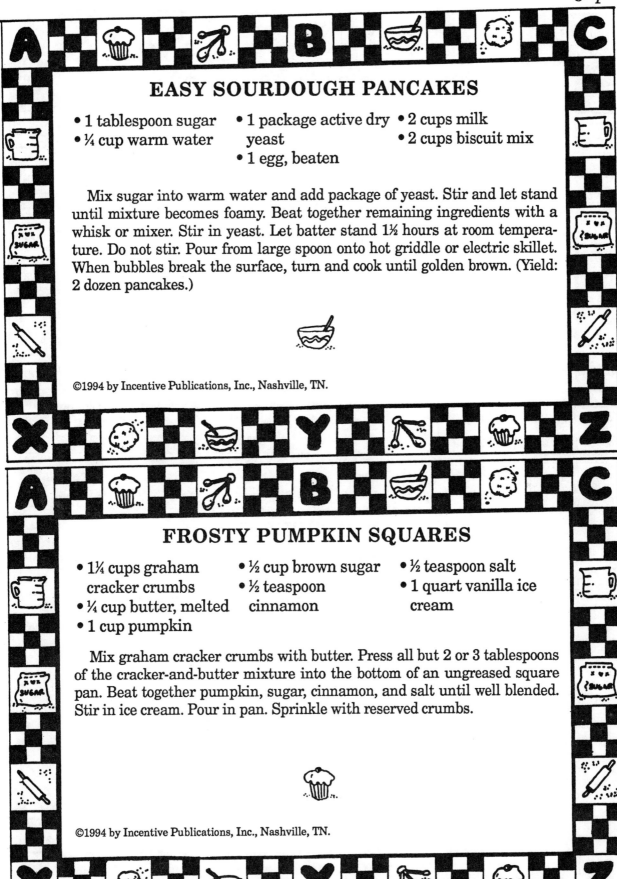

EASY SOURDOUGH PANCAKES

- 1 tablespoon sugar
- ¼ cup warm water
- 1 package active dry yeast
- 1 egg, beaten
- 2 cups milk
- 2 cups biscuit mix

Mix sugar into warm water and add package of yeast. Stir and let stand until mixture becomes foamy. Beat together remaining ingredients with a whisk or mixer. Stir in yeast. Let batter stand 1½ hours at room temperature. Do not stir. Pour from large spoon onto hot griddle or electric skillet. When bubbles break the surface, turn and cook until golden brown. (Yield: 2 dozen pancakes.)

FROSTY PUMPKIN SQUARES

- 1¼ cups graham cracker crumbs
- ¼ cup butter, melted
- 1 cup pumpkin
- ½ cup brown sugar
- ½ teaspoon cinnamon
- ½ teaspoon salt
- 1 quart vanilla ice cream

Mix graham cracker crumbs with butter. Press all but 2 or 3 tablespoons of the cracker-and-butter mixture into the bottom of an ungreased square pan. Beat together pumpkin, sugar, cinnamon, and salt until well blended. Stir in ice cream. Pour in pan. Sprinkle with reserved crumbs.

GORP (GOOD OLD RAISINS AND PEANUTS)

- sunflower seeds
- pumpkin seeds
- raisins or other chopped dried fruit
- chocolate chips
- peanuts or other chopped nuts
- shredded coconut

Mix together as much of the ingredients that you desire. Store in a plastic container. Eat this trail mix when hiking, walking, or biking.

A   B   C

HUSHPUPPIES

- 2 cups yellow cornmeal
- 1 cup flour
- 2 tablespoons baking powder
- 2 tablespoons sugar
- 2 teaspoons salt
- 2 teaspoons baking soda
- 1¾ cups buttermilk
- 1 egg
- oil for frying

Mix together cornmeal, flour, baking powder, sugar, salt, and baking soda. Add buttermilk and egg. Beat well. Batter will be thick. Cover and let stand at room temperature for 1 hour. Batter may be refrigerated for up to 14 hours. Heat 1½″ oil to 325° in heavy skillet. Drop batter by tablespoonfuls and cook about 3 minutes, turning twice. Drain on paper towels. (Yield: 5 dozen hushpuppies.)

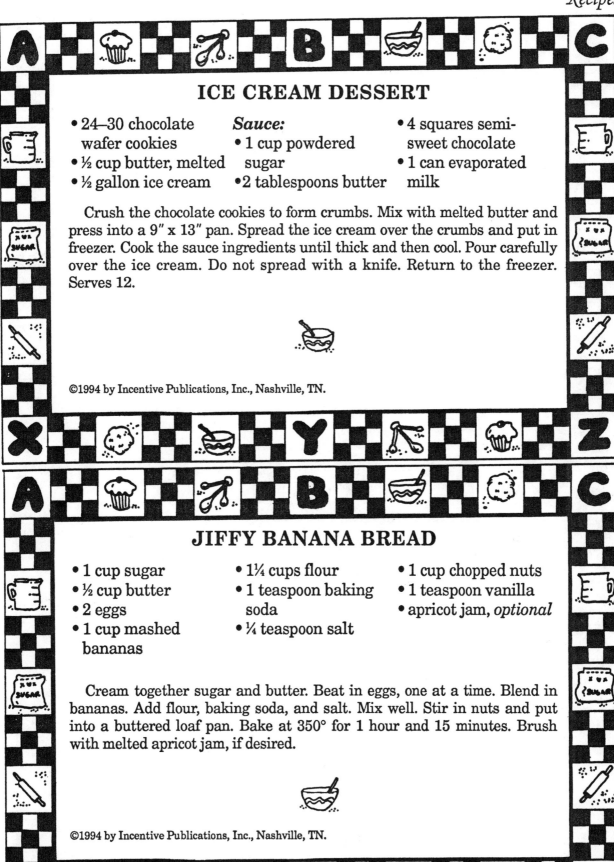

ICE CREAM DESSERT

- 24–30 chocolate wafer cookies
- ½ cup butter, melted
- ½ gallon ice cream

Sauce:
- 1 cup powdered sugar
- 2 tablespoons butter

- 4 squares semi-sweet chocolate
- 1 can evaporated milk

Crush the chocolate cookies to form crumbs. Mix with melted butter and press into a 9″ x 13″ pan. Spread the ice cream over the crumbs and put in freezer. Cook the sauce ingredients until thick and then cool. Pour carefully over the ice cream. Do not spread with a knife. Return to the freezer. Serves 12.

©1994 by Incentive Publications, Inc., Nashville, TN.

JIFFY BANANA BREAD

- 1 cup sugar
- ½ cup butter
- 2 eggs
- 1 cup mashed bananas

- 1¼ cups flour
- 1 teaspoon baking soda
- ¼ teaspoon salt

- 1 cup chopped nuts
- 1 teaspoon vanilla
- apricot jam, *optional*

Cream together sugar and butter. Beat in eggs, one at a time. Blend in bananas. Add flour, baking soda, and salt. Mix well. Stir in nuts and put into a buttered loaf pan. Bake at 350° for 1 hour and 15 minutes. Brush with melted apricot jam, if desired.

©1994 by Incentive Publications, Inc., Nashville, TN.

KABOBS

- pickle slices
- cherry tomatoes
- pineapple chunks
- cheese cubes
- cucumber wedges
- olives

Place a mixture of the fruits, cheeses, and vegetables on wooden skewers in colorful combinations. Can be served alone or with a dip.

A B C

LUMBERJACK LOGS

- 1 cup creamy peanut butter
- ¾ to 1 cup honey
- 1 cup instant nonfat dry milk
- 1 cup raisins
- 1 cup graham cracker crumbs

Blend together peanut butter, honey, and dry milk. Chop raisins and add to mixture. (Add 1 teaspoon oil to raisins for easier chopping.) Mix thoroughly. Add graham cracker crumbs and mix well. Using a teaspoon, drop on waxed paper. Roll to form logs and chill. Makes about 60.

X Y Z

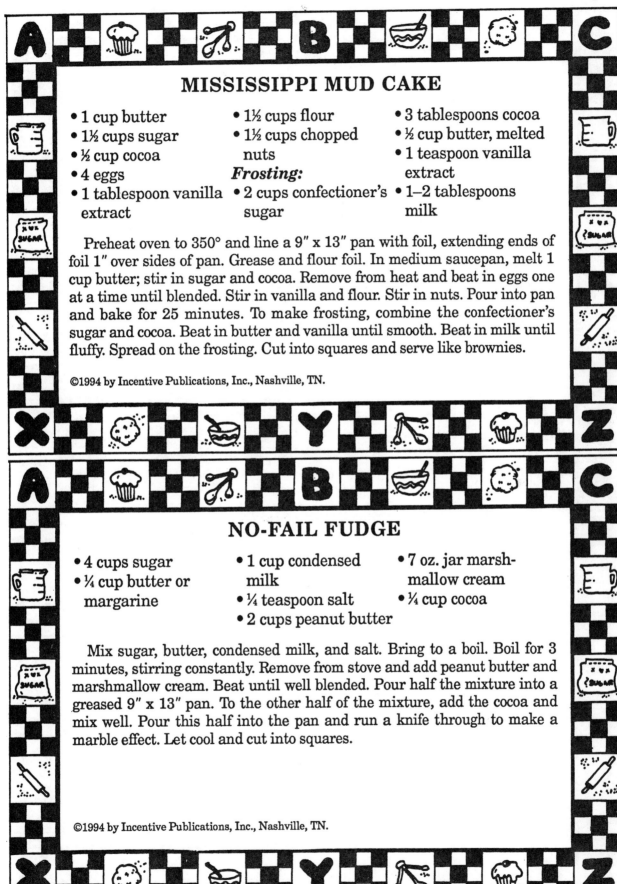

MISSISSIPPI MUD CAKE

- 1 cup butter
- 1½ cups sugar
- ½ cup cocoa
- 4 eggs
- 1 tablespoon vanilla extract

- 1½ cups flour
- 1½ cups chopped nuts

Frosting:
- 2 cups confectioner's sugar

- 3 tablespoons cocoa
- ½ cup butter, melted
- 1 teaspoon vanilla extract
- 1–2 tablespoons milk

Preheat oven to 350° and line a 9" x 13" pan with foil, extending ends of foil 1" over sides of pan. Grease and flour foil. In medium saucepan, melt 1 cup butter; stir in sugar and cocoa. Remove from heat and beat in eggs one at a time until blended. Stir in vanilla and flour. Stir in nuts. Pour into pan and bake for 25 minutes. To make frosting, combine the confectioner's sugar and cocoa. Beat in butter and vanilla until smooth. Beat in milk until fluffy. Spread on the frosting. Cut into squares and serve like brownies.

NO-FAIL FUDGE

- 4 cups sugar
- ¼ cup butter or margarine

- 1 cup condensed milk
- ¼ teaspoon salt
- 2 cups peanut butter

- 7 oz. jar marsh- mallow cream
- ¼ cup cocoa

Mix sugar, butter, condensed milk, and salt. Bring to a boil. Boil for 3 minutes, stirring constantly. Remove from stove and add peanut butter and marshmallow cream. Beat until well blended. Pour half the mixture into a greased 9" x 13" pan. To the other half of the mixture, add the cocoa and mix well. Pour this half into the pan and run a knife through to make a marble effect. Let cool and cut into squares.

OATMEAL CHOCOLATE CHIP BARS

- 1½ cups brown sugar, packed firm
- ¾ cup sugar
- 1 cup vegetable shortening
- 3 eggs

- 1 teaspoon vanilla extract
- 1¼ cups flour
- 1 teaspoon baking soda
- 1 teaspoon salt

- 1½ teaspoons cinnamon
- ¾ cup milk
- 4 cups rolled oats, uncooked
- 1 bag (12 oz.) chocolate chips

Blend sugars into vegetable shortening and gradually beat in eggs and vanilla extract. Add flour, baking soda, salt, and cinnamon alternately with the milk. Stir in the remaining ingredients. Spread batter into a greased pan and bake at 350° for about 30 minutes. Cut while warm, but cool completely in pan before lifting out.

PUPPY CHOW FOR PEOPLE

- 4 cups corn cereal
- 4 cups bran cereal
- ¾ cup peanut butter

- 1 stick margarine
- 1 cup chocolate chips

- 2½ cups powdered sugar

Mix cereal in a large bowl. Melt the peanut butter, margarine, and chocolate chips in a glass bowl in the microwave or over low heat on the stove. Pour over cereal. Put powdered sugar in a large brown paper bag, add the cereal, and shake until well coated. Store in the refrigerator. Can be kept for up to 3 weeks.

QUICK-AS-A-WINK COFFEE RING

- 1 tube refrigerator rolls
- 1 stick margarine, melted
- ¾ cup cinnamon and sugar mixture
- 1 cup raisins
- ½ cup ready-to-spread icing

Roll dough to form a rectangle ¼″ thick. Spread with melted butter, cinnamon-sugar, and raisins. Roll dough as you would a jelly roll, joining ends to form a ring. Slash top of ring at 2″ intervals. Let rise to twice the original size. Bake at 350° for 20–30 minutes. Top with icing.

RICE PUDDING

- 2 eggs
- ⅓ cup sugar
- ¼ teaspoon salt
- 2¾ cups flour
- 2 cups milk, scalded
- ½ teaspoon vanilla extract
- ¾ cup cooked rice
- cinnamon

Beat eggs, sugar, salt, flour, and scalded milk. Stir vanilla and rice into egg mixture. Sprinkle with cinnamon and bake at 350° for 40 minutes.

SCONES

- ¾ cup flour
- ½ teaspoon baking soda
- ½ teaspoon cream of tartar
- ¼ cup sugar
- 1 egg
- ¾ cup milk plus 1 tablespoon vinegar

Mix together all ingredients in a blender and pour scones about the size of half an orange onto a greased griddle. Turn when full of bubbles.

TURTLES

- 1 bag caramel candies
- ¼ cup heavy cream
- 3 cups pecan halves
- 1 small package chocolate chips

In a saucepan, melt the caramels and heavy cream. Stir until smooth. Remove from heat and grease a jelly roll pan or cookie sheet. For each turtle, arrange four pecan halves on greased cookie sheet to form turtle's legs. Split one nut in half lengthwise and set one sliver at the top to represent the turtle's head and one at the bottom to represent its tail. Drip a spoonful of hot caramel over center of pecans. Tips of the turtle's feet, head, and tail should poke out of caramel covering. Let turtles sit untouched until caramel hardens. While turtles are firm, place chocolate bits in a saucepan, melt over low heat, and spoon a little melted chocolate over the back of each turtle. Let stand until chocolate is hard.

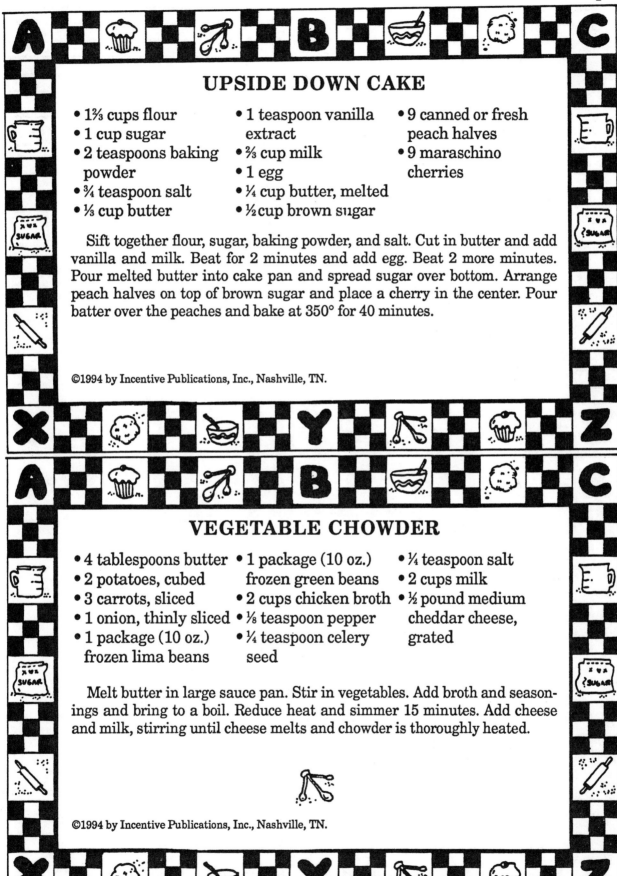

UPSIDE DOWN CAKE

- 1⅔ cups flour
- 1 cup sugar
- 2 teaspoons baking powder
- ¾ teaspoon salt
- ⅓ cup butter
- 1 teaspoon vanilla extract
- ⅔ cup milk
- 1 egg
- ¼ cup butter, melted
- ½ cup brown sugar
- 9 canned or fresh peach halves
- 9 maraschino cherries

Sift together flour, sugar, baking powder, and salt. Cut in butter and add vanilla and milk. Beat for 2 minutes and add egg. Beat 2 more minutes. Pour melted butter into cake pan and spread sugar over bottom. Arrange peach halves on top of brown sugar and place a cherry in the center. Pour batter over the peaches and bake at 350° for 40 minutes.

VEGETABLE CHOWDER

- 4 tablespoons butter
- 2 potatoes, cubed
- 3 carrots, sliced
- 1 onion, thinly sliced
- 1 package (10 oz.) frozen lima beans
- 1 package (10 oz.) frozen green beans
- 2 cups chicken broth
- ⅛ teaspoon pepper
- ¼ teaspoon celery seed
- ¼ teaspoon salt
- 2 cups milk
- ½ pound medium cheddar cheese, grated

Melt butter in large sauce pan. Stir in vegetables. Add broth and seasonings and bring to a boil. Reduce heat and simmer 15 minutes. Add cheese and milk, stirring until cheese melts and chowder is thoroughly heated.

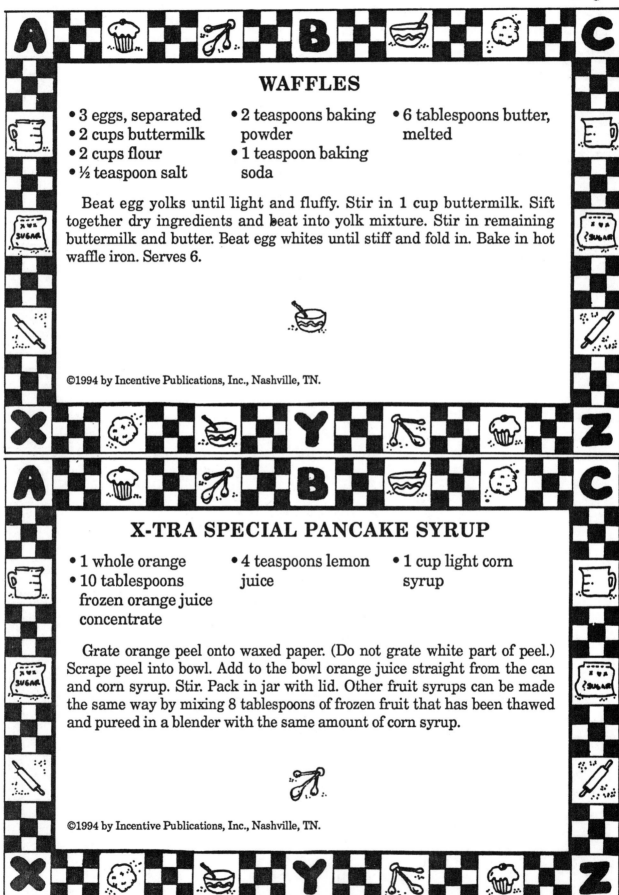

WAFFLES

- 3 eggs, separated
- 2 cups buttermilk
- 2 cups flour
- ½ teaspoon salt
- 2 teaspoons baking powder
- 1 teaspoon baking soda
- 6 tablespoons butter, melted

Beat egg yolks until light and fluffy. Stir in 1 cup buttermilk. Sift together dry ingredients and beat into yolk mixture. Stir in remaining buttermilk and butter. Beat egg whites until stiff and fold in. Bake in hot waffle iron. Serves 6.

X-TRA SPECIAL PANCAKE SYRUP

- 1 whole orange
- 10 tablespoons frozen orange juice concentrate
- 4 teaspoons lemon juice
- 1 cup light corn syrup

Grate orange peel onto waxed paper. (Do not grate white part of peel.) Scrape peel into bowl. Add to the bowl orange juice straight from the can and corn syrup. Stir. Pack in jar with lid. Other fruit syrups can be made the same way by mixing 8 tablespoons of frozen fruit that has been thawed and pureed in a blender with the same amount of corn syrup.

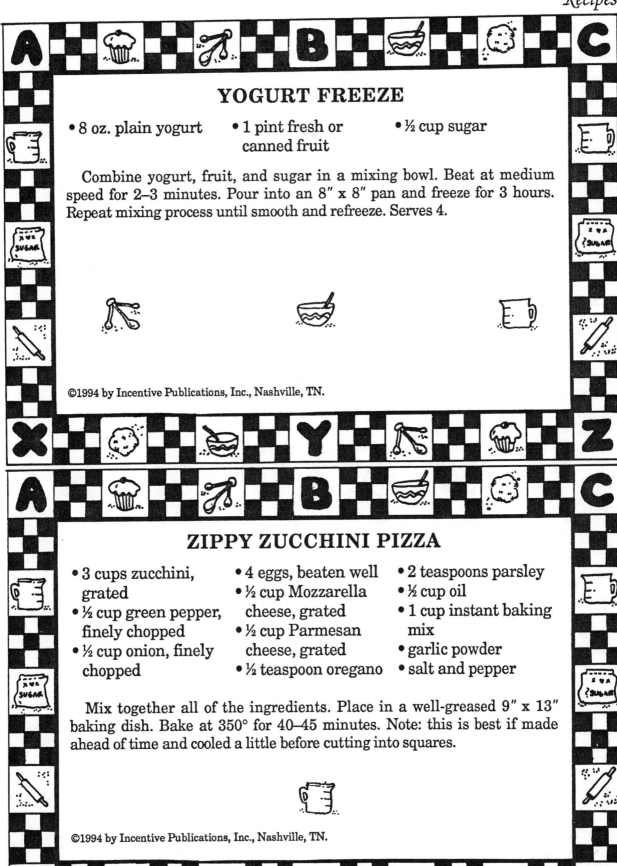

YOGURT FREEZE

- 8 oz. plain yogurt
- 1 pint fresh or canned fruit
- ½ cup sugar

Combine yogurt, fruit, and sugar in a mixing bowl. Beat at medium speed for 2–3 minutes. Pour into an 8″ x 8″ pan and freeze for 3 hours. Repeat mixing process until smooth and refreeze. Serves 4.

ZIPPY ZUCCHINI PIZZA

- 3 cups zucchini, grated
- ½ cup green pepper, finely chopped
- ½ cup onion, finely chopped
- 4 eggs, beaten well
- ½ cup Mozzarella cheese, grated
- ½ cup Parmesan cheese, grated
- ½ teaspoon oregano
- 2 teaspoons parsley
- ½ cup oil
- 1 cup instant baking mix
- garlic powder
- salt and pepper

Mix together all of the ingredients. Place in a well-greased 9″ x 13″ baking dish. Bake at 350° for 40–45 minutes. Note: this is best if made ahead of time and cooled a little before cutting into squares.

Storybook

Creative dramatics and personal interpretation of literature is key to helping children understand and assimilate what they read, as well as to relate it to their own lives in a meaningful way. By reading and interpreting popular children's stories, your young students will be able to develop their imaginations and extend their language skills.

■ The recipes on the following pages are to be used in conjunction with the variety of storybooks listed on page 113 and popular nursery rhymes. Be creative with your implementation of these recipes in the day's curriculum. For example, when reading the story of *The Gingerbread Man* by Karen Schmidt, let your students mix up a batch of **Gingerbread Men** cookie dough (page 116). Guide the students to build one giant Gingerbread Man by directing each student to add a

piece of dough to either the head, arms, legs, or body. Raisins can be added for the eyes and buttons can be added to his waistcoat.

■ After the Gingerbread Man has finished baking, hide him from the children and leave a clue to his whereabouts inside the oven. When you take your students to retrieve the cookie, they will find the clue and begin their hunt. Your hunt can be as simple or as elaborate as you wish it; the only stipulation should be that the students are challenged and excited enough by the clues to engage in problem-solving and language arts activities. You may want to leaves clues with different members of the school community: the principal, the nurse, the gym teacher, the librarian, etc. A sample clue might be:

> I've jumped from the oven, now what do you think?
>
> I've run down the hall as quick as a wink!
>
> Now start your thinking, and try not to stall.
>
> I'm in the room of the man who's in charge of us all.

OTHER BOOKS FOR STORYBOOK

The Adventures of Pinocchio by Carlo Collodi.

Alice's Adventures in Wonderland by Lewis Carroll.

A Bear Called Paddington by Michael Bond.

Chicken Soup with Rice by Maurice Sendak.

Clifford, the Big Red Dog by Norman Bridwell.

Curious George by H.A. Rey.

Heidi by Johanna Spyri.

Peter Pan and Wendy by James M. Barrie.

Stone Soup by Marcia Brown.

BILLY GOATS GRUFF SALAD

- 1 head lettuce, coarsely chopped
- 3 stalks celery, finely chopped
- 1 green pepper, chopped
- 1 onion, thinly sliced
- 1 package (10 oz.) frozen peas
- 1 pint mayonnaise
- 3 tablespoons sugar
- 6 oz. Parmesan cheese, grated

Place chopped lettuce in the bottom of a large bowl. One layer at a time, place the other vegetables on top of the lettuce. Mix mayonnaise and sugar and spread over the top of the last layer. Sprinkle with Parmesan cheese. Refrigerate before serving and toss when ready to eat.

DOGGIE BONE COOKIES

- ⅓ cup butter or margarine
- ⅔ cup sugar
- 1 egg
- 1 teaspoon vanilla extract
- 2½ cups sifted flour
- ½ teaspoon salt

Cream butter and sugar. Beat in egg and vanilla. In separate bowl, combine the flour and salt and then mix with the butter mixture. Chill dough for at least 3 hours. Preheat oven to 350°. On floured surface, roll out dough to ⅛″ thickness and cut into shapes. Bake cookies on a greased cookie sheet for about 8 minutes.

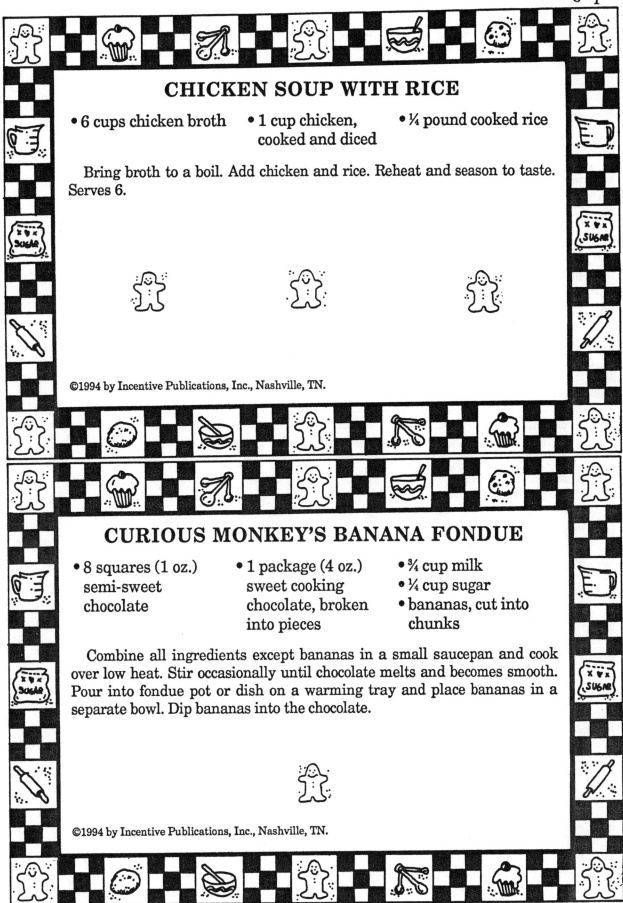

CHICKEN SOUP WITH RICE

- 6 cups chicken broth
- 1 cup chicken, cooked and diced
- ¼ pound cooked rice

Bring broth to a boil. Add chicken and rice. Reheat and season to taste. Serves 6.

CURIOUS MONKEY'S BANANA FONDUE

- 8 squares (1 oz.) semi-sweet chocolate
- 1 package (4 oz.) sweet cooking chocolate, broken into pieces
- ¾ cup milk
- ¼ cup sugar
- bananas, cut into chunks

Combine all ingredients except bananas in a small saucepan and cook over low heat. Stir occasionally until chocolate melts and becomes smooth. Pour into fondue pot or dish on a warming tray and place bananas in a separate bowl. Dip bananas into the chocolate.

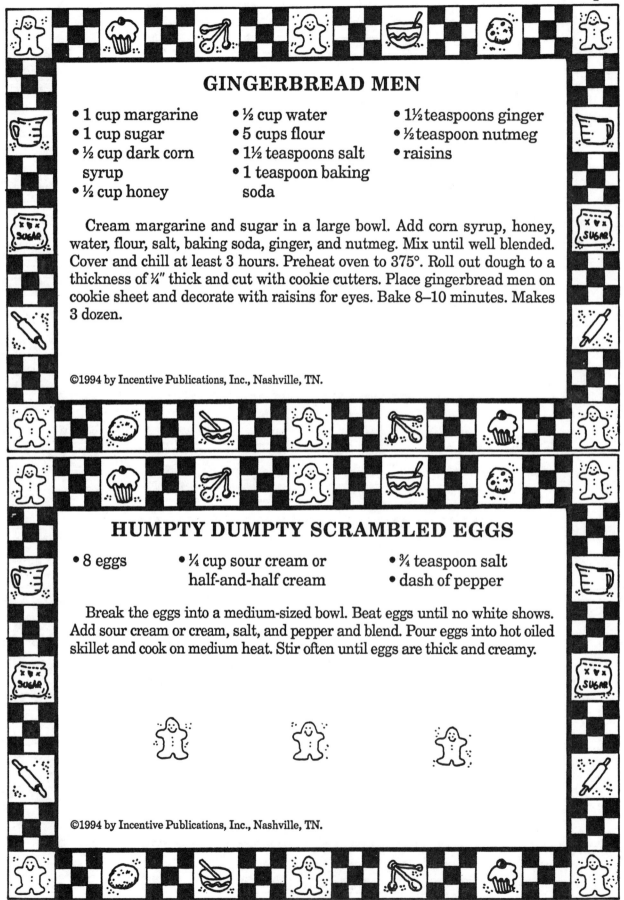

GINGERBREAD MEN

- 1 cup margarine
- 1 cup sugar
- ½ cup dark corn syrup
- ½ cup honey
- ½ cup water
- 5 cups flour
- 1½ teaspoons salt
- 1 teaspoon baking soda
- 1½ teaspoons ginger
- ½ teaspoon nutmeg
- raisins

Cream margarine and sugar in a large bowl. Add corn syrup, honey, water, flour, salt, baking soda, ginger, and nutmeg. Mix until well blended. Cover and chill at least 3 hours. Preheat oven to 375°. Roll out dough to a thickness of ¼" thick and cut with cookie cutters. Place gingerbread men on cookie sheet and decorate with raisins for eyes. Bake 8–10 minutes. Makes 3 dozen.

HUMPTY DUMPTY SCRAMBLED EGGS

- 8 eggs
- ¼ cup sour cream or half-and-half cream
- ¾ teaspoon salt
- dash of pepper

Break the eggs into a medium-sized bowl. Beat eggs until no white shows. Add sour cream or cream, salt, and pepper and blend. Pour eggs into hot oiled skillet and cook on medium heat. Stir often until eggs are thick and creamy.

MOUNTAIN TOP TOASTED CHEESE SANDWICHES

- 2 eggs
- ¾ cup milk
- ½ teaspoon salt

- 8 slices American cheese
- 8 slices white bread

- 4 tablespoons butter

Crack the eggs and beat them slightly using a fork. Stir in milk and salt. Make the cheese sandwiches by putting two slices of cheese between two slices of bread. Melt 2 tablespoons butter in skillet and heat. Dip the sandwiches on both sides in the egg-and-milk mixture. Let them soak a minute and then brown sandwiches on both sides. Serves 4.

JACK AND THE BEAN STALK GREEN BEANS

- 1 pound green beans, snapped or canned

- 1 medium tomato
- ½ cup onion, chopped

- 1 teaspoon salt
- dash of pepper
- 2 tablespoons butter

Combine all ingredients in a skillet. Cook until beans are tender.

LITTLE BO PEEP'S SHEEP

• large marshmallows   • shredded coconut

Place marshmallows in a slotted spoon and dip them quickly into a pot of boiling water. Roll marshmallows in shredded coconut. Place on waxed paper to dry.

LITTLE RED HEN'S BREAD

• 2 packages active yeast
• ¼ cup sugar
• ½ cup warm water
• 1 cup milk
• ½ cup shortening
• 3 eggs, beaten
• ½ cup sugar
• 6–7 cups flour
• 1½ teaspoons salt

Combine yeast, sugar, and water. Let stand 5 minutes. Scald milk and add shortening. Cool. Stir in eggs, sugar, and yeast. Beat in 2 cups flour and salt. Continue beating in flour until dough is not sticky. Knead 10 more minutes. Place in greased bowl and cover with tea towel. Let rise until dough has doubled in size (about 1½ hours). Punch down and make into loaves. Let rise 40 more minutes and bake at 375° for 35–40 minutes.

THREE BEARS' PORRIDGE

- 2 cups rolled oats
- 4 cups water
- ¼ teaspoon salt
- 1 teaspoon butter

Stir oats into briskly boiling salted water. Add butter and cook 5 minutes, stirring occasionally. Cover and remove from heat. Let stand for several minutes more. Serve with honey, maple syrup, or brown sugar. Top with milk. Serves 6.

LITTLE BEAR'S HONEY BUTTER
AND CINNAMON TOAST

Honey Butter:
- 4 tablespoons butter or margarine
- 1 tablespoon honey

Cinnamon Toast:
- 4 slices bread
- 1 teaspoon cinnamon
- 3 tablespoons granulated sugar

To make the honey butter, mix together the butter and honey. Stir until butter is fluffy. To make the cinnamon toast, mix together the cinnamon and sugar and store in a glass jar. Toast the bread, spread with honey butter, and sprinkle with the cinnamon-sugar mixture. Serves 4.

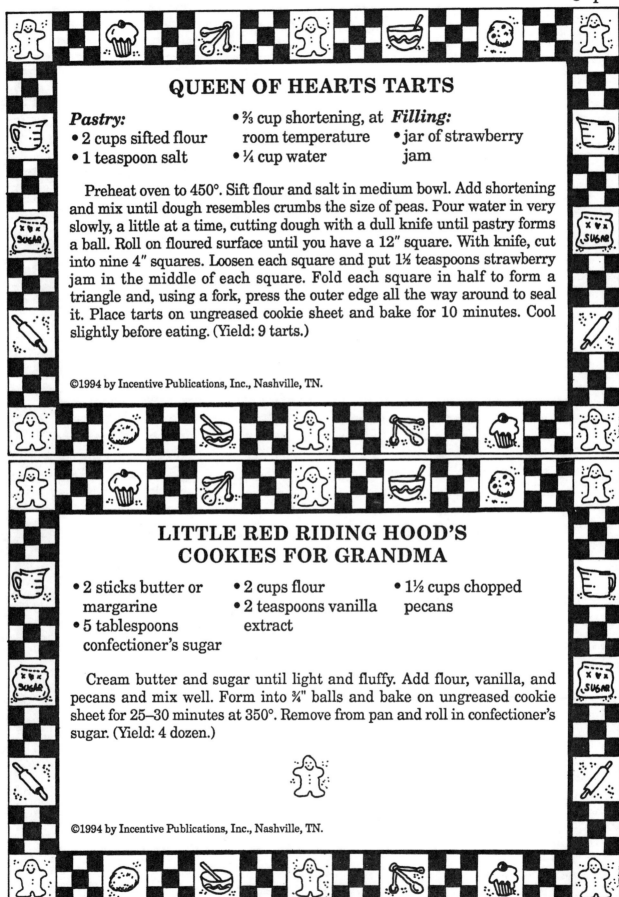

QUEEN OF HEARTS TARTS

Pastry:
- 2 cups sifted flour
- 1 teaspoon salt
- ⅔ cup shortening, at room temperature
- ¼ cup water

Filling:
- jar of strawberry jam

Preheat oven to 450°. Sift flour and salt in medium bowl. Add shortening and mix until dough resembles crumbs the size of peas. Pour water in very slowly, a little at a time, cutting dough with a dull knife until pastry forms a ball. Roll on floured surface until you have a 12″ square. With knife, cut into nine 4″ squares. Loosen each square and put 1½ teaspoons strawberry jam in the middle of each square. Fold each square in half to form a triangle and, using a fork, press the outer edge all the way around to seal it. Place tarts on ungreased cookie sheet and bake for 10 minutes. Cool slightly before eating. (Yield: 9 tarts.)

LITTLE RED RIDING HOOD'S
COOKIES FOR GRANDMA

- 2 sticks butter or margarine
- 5 tablespoons confectioner's sugar
- 2 cups flour
- 2 teaspoons vanilla extract
- 1½ cups chopped pecans

Cream butter and sugar until light and fluffy. Add flour, vanilla, and pecans and mix well. Form into ¾″ balls and bake on ungreased cookie sheet for 25–30 minutes at 350°. Remove from pan and roll in confectioner's sugar. (Yield: 4 dozen.)

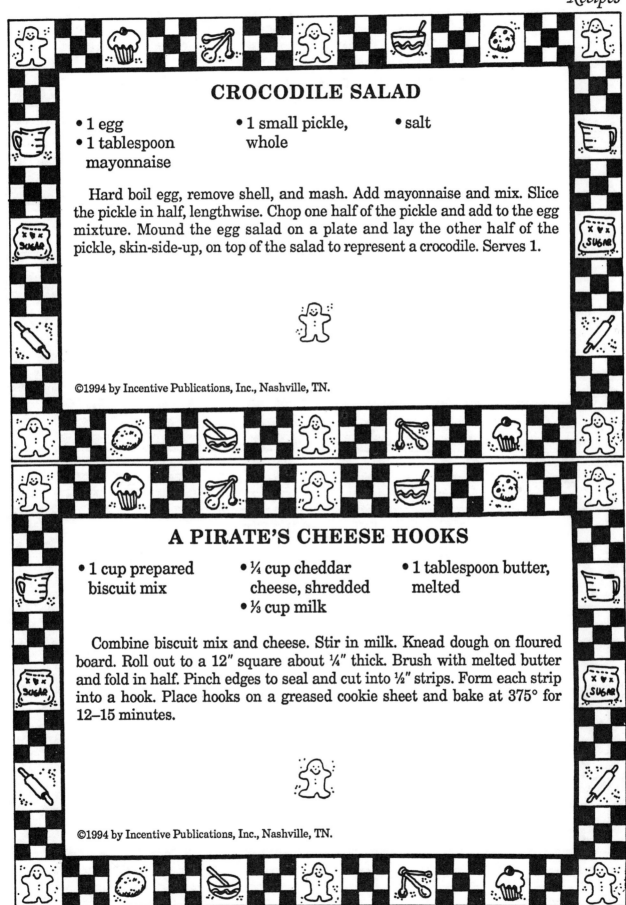

CROCODILE SALAD

- 1 egg
- 1 tablespoon mayonnaise
- 1 small pickle, whole
- salt

Hard boil egg, remove shell, and mash. Add mayonnaise and mix. Slice the pickle in half, lengthwise. Chop one half of the pickle and add to the egg mixture. Mound the egg salad on a plate and lay the other half of the pickle, skin-side-up, on top of the salad to represent a crocodile. Serves 1.

A PIRATE'S CHEESE HOOKS

- 1 cup prepared biscuit mix
- ¼ cup cheddar cheese, shredded
- ⅓ cup milk
- 1 tablespoon butter, melted

Combine biscuit mix and cheese. Stir in milk. Knead dough on floured board. Roll out to a 12″ square about ¼″ thick. Brush with melted butter and fold in half. Pinch edges to seal and cut into ½″ strips. Form each strip into a hook. Place hooks on a greased cookie sheet and bake at 375° for 12–15 minutes.

NEVER-TELL-A-LIE BISCUITS

- 1 package yeast
- 1 cup lukewarm water
- 4 tablespoons soft butter
- 1 tablespoon sugar
- 1 teaspoon salt
- 2½ cups flour
- 1 egg white

Dissolve yeast in warm water and let stand for 5 minutes. Stir in butter, sugar, and salt. Gradually beat in the flour. Continue to beat 5 minutes by hand, adding more flour if necessary in order to make dough firm enough to handle. Knead dough and roll into a 8″ x 12″ rectangle. Cut rectangle in half and then cut each half into 8 short strips. Roll each strip into ropes about 10″ long. Place on a cookie sheet at least 1″ apart and let rise 15 minutes. Brush with egg white and bake for 5 minutes at 425° and then for 15 minutes at 350°.

GARDEN SOUP

- 2 or 3 well-washed stones
- 3 quarts chicken broth
- carrots, chopped
- celery, chopped
- potatoes, chopped
- onion, chopped
- tomatoes, canned or fresh
- corn

Put the stones in a large pot and add chicken broth and various chopped vegetables. Simmer until vegetables are tender.

Index